IN THE BEGINNING
A HEAD START TO A STRONG FINISH

VERNON GORDON

Table of Contents:

FIRST THINGS FIRST:
Frequently Asked Questions About Living as a Christian

THE ESSENTIALS:
Building Blocks for a Strong Spiritual Foundation

Dedication:

This book is dedicated my wife, Ashley, and my two children Madison and Jackson, who inspire me each day to be a better man. To my family who through experience, honesty, and love have pulled out of me the potential inside. To Danielle, who's been my sister, editor, cheerleader, and accountability partner since the beginning of my process. To my Spring Creek Baptist Church family, who allowed me the space to grow and develop for so many years. To my Life Church family who honors me with the privilege of being their pastor and has supported me watering every seed God has placed inside me. And finally, to the ones who inspired this work originally, the VCU student body and Drop Zone community. Your transparency, discipleship, belief in me, and friendships have molded this work and I am grateful to God for the opportunity to have served you. Thank you to you all.

THE INTRO CHAPTER
BUILDING SOMETHING THAT CAN LAST

The night was just for me! Every word spoken pierced my side and made me wonder if the speaker had been sitting in my bedroom behind closed doors witnessing my every secret. The lights were dim, music echoing softly in the background, his voice piercing the silence moving my emotions and picking apart my thoughts. Overcome with a rush of both conviction and attraction to this relationship I had always been around but had never personally experienced I mustered up the courage to stand up! Invited, I took a step into the aisle and walked down to repeat the words of the preacher, "I confess with my mouth, and believe in my heart, that Jesus died on the cross for my sins and rose again! I am saved!" And I felt.....FREE! Well for a moment!

Shortly after this invigorating experience, we arrived home to this "new life" I had just obtained. Just an adolescent at the time, I closed my door, and that newfound freedom quickly turned into newfound questions! I said, *"I believe in Jesus Christ, but didn't I always believe that?"* I said, *"I believe he died on the cross for my sins and rose again, but didn't I always believe that?"* I said, *"I'm saved", but what does that even mean? Saved from what?"* I was wrestling with this crash from the emotionalism that I had just experienced an hour before and the present reality I felt which was so different from the church experience. Wrestling with thoughts like *"I don't 'feel' different; should I?"* And that freedom I had experienced just moments prior was arrested by a question that would shadow me over and over again as I took that same walk more times than I can count. What now?

Standing at the beginning of a new journey can be exciting on one hand while terrifying on the other! Kind of like those flight jackets I wore in middle school that was orange on the inside and black on the outside. Sometimes this journey will find you trying to define your Christianity. Some of the definitions one might encounter could say it is a baptized believer, while others would suggest it is one who lives out the commandments of the Bible to the best of their ability, and even another might say it is one who fulfills the obligation of Romans 10:9-10. Or maybe we just have to look for those "Fruits of the Spirit" that Christians should possess in their daily lives? While all of these are a snapshot of the life of a believer, they provide little support to the practical implementation of a believer's lifestyle. And more importantly, they fail to answer the big question of "Why"? Christianity gives us surprising answers as to what it requires: fasting, give away your money to a church, love people who hate you. However, none of these things sounded particularly appealing to me as I began my spiritual journey. In full transparency, sometimes they still don't. The truth is I think we all know persons who've been baptized, who made confessions and are exceptionally well versed in biblical dialect, yet we struggle to see the difference between their lifestyle and that of those we know have not fulfilled these obligations. This undefined territory is where we often find ourselves on our journey, seeking clarity on what model to follow to achieve spiritual growth and transformation. With so many ideas and opinions under the same name of religion, serving the same God, the truth is it can be difficult to differentiate at times. Often this struggle kills the momentum of the Christian journey before your feet even hit the ground running.

Now I know I've lost a group of readers already who've said through the first two paragraphs, "I'm not a new believer, but I know someone this would be great for!" I wouldn't dare argue with you about your Christianity, that's between you and God. But I would challenge you to think about your "beginnings" before you put this book in your closet and regret ever picking it up. Jesus says in Luke 6:48, *"It is like a person building a house who digs deep and lays the foundation on solid rock. When the floodwaters rise and break against that house, it stands firm because it is well built."* This is the type of spiritual foundation God would desire us to have, one that is firm, sincere, and built to last. The real objective of this book is not just for those who are new to faith but to help all of us evaluate our foundations, and to see how we can fortify our Christian experience. Remember that story of the Three Little Pigs? One pig built his house out of straw, and the wolf easily blew it down. Another out of clay, and it also was destroyed without considerable strain by the wolf. But the last little piggy built his house out of brick, and because its foundation was strong, it could not be blown down. He not only secured what he valued by building on the solid foundation, but he became a refuge to his brothers in their time of need. I hope that upon reading this book you'll join me on a journey we all should take to become the third "Little Piggy"! Whether you've grown up in church or are being introduced to some of these concepts for the first time, I pray you find both clarity and constructive conviction in the words on these pages. Each chapter is designed to bring forth practical revelations about foundational principles related to faith development. There is no "one-size-fits-all" on this journey. But each step forward brings more independence, new interest, and challenges. So let's commit to a beautiful journey. A head start, and ultimately, a strong finish.

The Intro Devotional

Luke 6:48
"It is like a person building a house who digs deep and lays the foundation on solid rock. When the floodwaters rise and break against that house, it stands firm because it is well built."

There's a story about a businessman who had a corner office on the top floor of his building. While very successful, he would come in day after day and feel like the building was rocking from side to side, swaying in the air. After attempting to ignore it, he consulted others who felt the instability all the same. They called an inspector to the property, and when he arrived, he started to walk to the basement. The businessman insisted he follow him stating, *"The problem is on the top floor."* The inspector replied, *"Sir if you're feeling unstable at the top, it's because something is wrong with the foundation."* This simple story is a beautiful reminder of the challenge we all have to create strong foundations. We all know too many stories of people who climbed the ladder, reached the top, only to attain what they could not sustain because of a foundational issue. Foundations are the heartbeat and healthiest way to find fulfillment in your Christian journey.

Reflection Questions:

If you had to rank your spiritual foundation from a 1 - 10, 1 being unstable and ten being stable, what would it be?

Has there been a time where you felt like your spiritual momentum declined? If so, when and what was the cause?

What's one area of your spiritual life that you know needs strengthening?

Inside-Out:

_____

_____

_____

_____

_____

_____

_____

_____

_____

_____

_____

_____

_____

Devotional Prayer

Today is a new day. It's a day I own and influence with my words, thoughts, and spirit. I am committed to building a strong foundation for my faith. I may not be perfect, but I will be passionate. I may not have all the answers, but I will have a great attitude. I may not be where I want to be, but I'm pushing towards the mark with confidence and consistency. Today I ask for protection against anything or anyone that does not align with my purpose. And I command my heart and mind to be open to your leading and guidance. I am excited about life, and this marks a new beginning.
In Jesus Name, Amen.

THE RELATIONSHIP VS. RELIGION CHAPTER

CREATING A POSITIVE PERSPECTIVE

Relationships are tricky, aren't they? I mean there's the constant struggle of communication and understanding, sacrifice and submission, idealistic versus what's realistic, and my personal favorite, the moments between the confident execution of a task and complete confusion at the response. Let me give you an example: It was Ashley, and I second year of marriage, and she had been saying she wanted me to help out more around the house. Her love language is "Acts of Service" so I thought and thought and then a light bulb went off. Later that week, I left the church office early and cut the grass, trimmed the edges (which I had never done in my life, so they were pretty bad), washed the car, washed the dishes, and pulled out my specialty meal; eggs, bacon, and biscuits for dinner! I found myself walking around the house singing *"I GOTTA FEELING, WOO-HOO! THAT TONIGHT'S GONNA BE A GOOD NIGHT!"* Ashley arrived home right on time, and after about thirty minutes I realized I had not received the response I was expecting. She hadn't mentioned any of it until she said one thing that made me lose it, *"Babe, you gotta start cooking more adult meals!"* You can imagine my discontent! I felt as if she disregarded all that I had just done for her that day. The next day I was praying, and God asked me a question, *"Why did you do it? For the 'reward' or the 'relationship'?"* It took me back for a second, and I couldn't answer honestly because, when I thought about it, I did all the right stuff for all the wrong reasons. Could it be that often we do all the "right stuff" for God, for all the wrong reasons? God then issued me a challenge I'll never forget. *"I want you to serve this relationship the best you can while willingly remaining abstinent."* Now I know the super-saved don't think preachers should think like this, and should just be excited when God speaks. But umm...*insert panic emoji face here*. I had a little difficulty with this spiritual assignment! I mean God I've already done this whole abstinent thing before marriage, didn't plan on going back to that place EVER! But I reluctantly exercised obedience, and at the end, God showed me something unusual. I wasn't supposed to cook, clean, and wash dishes for a reward. I wasn't even supposed to do it because of my relationship with Ashley. I'm called to serve my wife because of my relationship with God. I had lost sight of how my first relationship could impact all of my relationships. When I love God to the best of my ability, it influences my responses, routine, attitude, and emotions. And if we learn to embrace this one word on our faith journey in its totality it can change the way we live our lives; Worship. Now I know you're thinking, Vernon that's too simple! But let's take the preconceived definition and images off of this word for a second and view it in its organic state.

THE HEART OF WORSHIP

Worship at its core is a deep-rooted adoration and devotion to something or someone. It does not appear in Sunday morning service when the right chords are played or when you lift your hands. It is not the slow song in the worship set, and it's not even when the preacher says all the "good stuff" that makes you want to change something in your life. While all these moments and experiences can produce greater worship in our lives, to limit worship to these momentary expressions of emotionalism is to box our relationship into a specific place, time, and activity. Instead, I'd like for us to consider worship as a lifestyle, and most importantly a conscious choice. Because worship is inevitable, but who and what we worship is a choice. Recently I was talking with a friend of mine who's getting married soon. He mentioned that he was on a business trip and some single women were flirting with him at this particular gathering. He asked me, *"Vernon, how do I avoid this as an engaged man? I don't have a ring on yet!"* I responded, *"A ring doesn't show your commitment, your lifestyle does that. People should see you are committed to someone by the way you interact with others, the boundaries you set, and the way you honor your relationship privately and publicly. Even when you're alone, they should see the reflection of your devotion!"* In other words, something should change about how we engage the world around us when we are committed to something or someone.

I think our relationship with God should have the same impact on our lives. When we start with relationship, we recognize that no matter where I am I want my life, my behavior, and my ethics to mirror my primary commitment. Challenging ourselves with daily devotion produces healthy habits in our lifestyle. What we worship highlights what we find to be a necessity or value in our lives. So when we say we can't live without something or someone, what we're saying is momentarily this is what I worship. For some of us it's our jobs throughout the week, our "boo's" and "bae's" on the weekends, and then we get to God on Sunday! Instead of saying worship should impact how I work throughout the week. Do I show up on time? Do I invest in producing great work? Do I model excellence and integrity? On the weekends am I investing time in healthy conversations with people and environments that can push me to a deeper place of social and spiritual success? Am I guarding my exposures? Am I conscious of my reputation? Because what worship seeks to do is impact the way we work, the way we socialize, the way we communicate, the way we live! Not just our Sunday mornings.

Now I want to be clear. Religion is not bad in and of itself. But religion alone is not the answer to the depth we all seek. It can lead you to the church, but only relationship can let the church work through you. Religion can learn songs, but only relationship allows lyrics to become anthems of the heart. Religion can have us open a Bible and memorize scriptures, but relationship makes those words reality in our walk. So don't run from religion, but don't rely on it either. Lean into the intimacy of God and find the joy in a relationship that's better than anything you've ever seen on earth.

The Relationship vs. Religion Devotional

Romans 12:1 (MSG)
So here's what I want you to do, God helping you: Take your everyday, ordinary life—your sleeping, eating, going-to-work, and walking-around life—and place it before God as an offering.

When I was a kid, my Mom and Dad would always say, "What you do when you leave this house is a reflection of your family." They were always instilling in me the importance of understanding I carry a name, and I represent more than myself. My grandfather who was the original Vernon Gordon was a prominent police Colonel in my hometown, and I can even recall being pulled over multiple times and after showing the officer my identification them echoing "You're Colonel Gordon's grandson? You know better." The connection to the family name was always with me. This simple truth is the same for all of us as carriers of God's name. Wherever we go, whether work, the gym, to dinner or a movie, we are always carriers of the name. May we always be sensitive to the joyful responsibility and reminded that worship happens all week long in all that we are and do.

Reflection Questions:

In your opinion, what is the most critical area of any relationship?

Looking at your answer to number 1, how secure is this area bet ween you and God?

In what practical ways will you worship God through your life this week?

Inside-Out:

_____
_____
_____
_____
_____
_____
_____
_____
_____
_____
_____
_____
_____
_____
_____

Devotional Prayer

Lord thank you for this day. Every moment I breathe is another opportunity to strengthen my relationship with you. Today I offer you my everyday life. I am committed to honoring you in how I work, treat people, speak, and even study. I pray that I am a carrier of your name and that others are transformed because of how I live. I will be intentional about viewing all I do today as worship. Thank you for this chance to grow in relationship with you. In Jesus Name Amen.

THE HOLINESS CHAPTER
WHAT DOES "CHRISTIAN" LOOK LIKE?

Recently I was at the gym and was asked by an employee what I did for a living?" After several guesses, I shared with her that I was a Pastor. Her face was priceless, and after a moment of disbelief she stuttered, *"...but you have tattoos, earrings, and you just don't look like a Pastor."* She went on to say, *"I've just never seen a Christian who looks like you!"* I left the gym that day with only one question replaying in my head, "What does a Christian look like?" I think you'll be pleased to hear three things I've found liberating about defining the Christian look. It was when I embraced these three principles that I saw my relationship with God beginning to grow exponentially: There's no one-size-fits-all approach. It's not a look, its a lifestyle! God wants your heart, not just a new habit! As we engage this chapter, I'll touch on each of these principles, and I hope that you find confidence in your Christianity.

THERE'S NO ONE-SIZE-FITS-ALL.

Living the "Christian Life" is a subjective conversation that has been the cause of much division. Many different views about the interpretation of scripture and spiritual obedience can emerge as we seek the same goal, pleasing God. I genuinely believe that most denominational perspectives aren't created with ill-intent, but ultimately out of a desire to see people be in right standing with God. With that being said, I think it's important to note that no one denomination or individual has all the answers. It's essential that we all rightly divide the words of scripture for ourselves and seek God's revelation in our lives. For clarity, there is a great need for finding wisdom in others, following good leadership, and asking questions, which I'll talk about in future chapters. Deciding how to construct your life in God can be a foreign or freestyle process at times. And while it would be easy for me to tell you "do this, this, that, and a little of what you see over there"....all it would create is behavior with no understanding. That type of programming can only last for so long. At some point, the mind and body want to know "Why"? Why can't I do this? Why can't I experience that? Why isn't it right for me to feel this way? Why can't I get this thing right? If these questions go unanswered or challenged too often, eventually curiosity will win the battle of the mind. The strongest type of discipleship is rooted in self-discovery, not dictatorship. It is only in having a strong, self-discovered Christianity that you'll find stability in your walk.

"Accept him whose faith is weak, without passing judgment on disputable matters... Who are you to judge someone else's servant? To his own master, he stands or falls. So then each of us will give an account of himself to God. So whatever you believe about these things keep between yourself and God." Romans 14:1,4,12,22

There will always be "disputable matters" when it comes to the conversation of righteous living. The truth is people have been arguing about appropriate behavior and boundaries since the initial spread of Christianity in the New Testament. Honestly, religious people spent a good portion of their time arguing with Jesus about what it meant to honor God with their life. This idea that we'll agree someday and find a "one-size-fits-all" Christianity has never been seen before. What's important is that you resist discouragement by way of judgment, opinions, and dogma as you find your way to God. Now, I don't want to make the mistake of misleading anyone into believing Christianity doesn't have standards and expectations. But I think one of the greatest dangers to progress is the constant challenge of spiritual comparison and commentary. Realize that you'll never look Christian enough to someone. And every great spiritual leader received commentary that was contrary to their call. Do me a favor! Make a conscious decision to make every day better than the last. Spiritual growth will happen as a result of consistency and intentionality, so find your pace and keep progressing. You only have your own race to run.

IT'S NOT A LOOK. IT'S A LIFESTYLE

Several years ago while still in seminary I witnessed a lecture on cultural independence. The communicator of the moment highlighted that every generation rebels in three ways; language, dress, and music. Growing adults seeking to have something they can call their own is a consistent reality of every generation. Interestingly enough, this becomes the battlefield in Christian dialogues as many of our faith traditions place a great deal of attention on specific areas as a way to advocate for "holiness." So let's look at that word for a bit, shall we? Holiness is defined as "to be separate or distinct". Holiness comes from an ancient word that meant, "to cut" or "to separate." But an even more accurate translation may be the phrase "a cut above the rest" in a modern context. In essence, real holiness is the distinction of more than just clothes, language, or music, but the distinction of character, integrity, work ethic, attitude, and lifestyle. It is to exemplify the highest level of standards and behavior in every environment we exist.

So let's step on some toes for a moment! (Including my own) Holiness ask a range of questions like, "Did you show up on time for work this week?", "Did you join in on spreading rumors about someone?", "Did you stop to share time with the person crying in the corner, or were you too busy for conversation?" True holiness ask the question, "Did my entire being honor God today?" and furthermore, "Was the God in me evident today to those around me?" My clothes, my attitude, my ethics, my giving, my compassion, my thinking, and my speech are all ways our lifestyle can highlight our relationship with God. If we're really living the life, we should look strange to others at times. That's what holiness is all about. GOD WANTS YOUR HEART, NOT JUST A NEW HABIT

Calculations show that 76% of persons in the United States of America consider themselves to be Christian. However, 3 out of every 5 Christians say they disconnect from their faith around the age of 15. (*study by the Barna Group, 2011)

80% of Christian-raised millennials will leave the faith for the first ten years of their adult life.

Just 56% of millennials (born 1990-1996) consider themselves to be Christian.

Only an estimated 24% of the US population will attend a worship service on Sunday mornings.

The religiously unaffiliated, including atheist and agnostics, now make up 23% of the US population

Interesting numbers to say the least. In a Bible study once I asked a large group of young adults *"How many of you all grew up in church most of your life?"* An overwhelming majority raised their hand without hesitation proud of their church roots. I then followed up and asked the question, *"Can someone name me the fruits of the spirit?"* After a period of silence team efforts were forged, but still, no one person or group of persons could recall them all. I then moved on to the "whole armor of God," and after much deliberation, one group hesitantly riddled them off. This pattern continued for topics such as the ten commandments and even the names of the twelve disciples in a room full of "church-bred believers."

Now I'm not judging one bit, but I was astonished at a reality that hit me that day. All too often we are "bred" into Christianity, losing the opportunity to forge genuine interest and passion towards a pursuit of understanding. Thus, biblical truths become diluted to word problems that we must memorize to pass religious tests for vacation Bible school and Sunday School. This classic moment reminds us that academic achievement, years of experience, or years of service do not exclude any of us from needing constant self-evaluation and further affirms the necessity for continuous growth and development. We have to break habits so that we can build hearts. In Matthew 15:8-9 we see these words: *"These people honor me with their lips, but their hearts are far from me. Their worship is a farce, for they teach human-made ideas as commands from God."* I would dare say this is a significant challenge still in the 21st century Christian. While trying to figure out the right thing to say, the right thing to do, the right way to look, the right way to be a Christian, we look for behavior modifications, not heart modifications. But that's why we refer to Christianity as being "born-again,"; because the goal of sincere Christianity is not to be cloned into someone else, but birthed into something original for God's molding. This process will transform you from the inside out, causing you to modify your appearance, your conversations, your social media image, your relationships, your appetite for addictions, because real change still comes from the inside out. A new habit will never change your life the way a new heart will.

In conclusion, start strong by forging your own journey. There are no shortcuts to a strong relationship in any facet of life, and God is no different. No one can give you all the answers, but if you can resist trying to "look" the part, and creating habits absent of your heart, you will find a beautiful relationship awaiting you. One that will touch every area of your being, as long as you build your habits from your heart. It's not the easiest way, but it will be the most fulfilling and sustainable way. Get it right "IN THE BEGINNING," and it'll make the rest of your journey a much sweeter experience.

The Holiness Devotional

1 Samuel 16:7 (NIV)
7 But the Lord said to Samuel, "Do not consider his appearance or his height, for I have rejected him. The Lord does not look at the things people look at. People look at the outward appearance, but the Lord looks at the heart."

I once heard a preacher say they should give out more Oscars at church than anywhere else because that's where the most action takes place. His point? We have become excellent "looking" churches, but under the surface, there are still a lot of hurts, pains, and brokenness that we cover we nice clothes and positive language. But the church is not a "look" or a "set group of phrases," it's a lifestyle that is personal and progressive. And while you may be off and running you're not racing anybody, so go at your own pace.I pray this is a reminder to you that you don't have a competing Christianity. Allow God to convict, correct, and communicate to you daily about how to better reflect his glory. But be confident in your own spiritual identity and calling, and follow God's voice, even when it leads you where no one has gone before. (Also read Psalm 139:23-24)

Reflection Questions:

Have you ever felt insecure in your walk with God? If so, in what ways?

What is one area of your life where you feel God calling you to greater sacrifice?

When you read Matthew 15:8-9, what do you see and hear? How does this apply to your life?

Inside-Out:

_____
_____
_____
_____
_____
_____
_____
_____
_____
_____
_____
_____
_____
_____
_____

Devotional Prayer

I am a Christian. I follow Christ and learn, daily, how to emulate his character and example better. I offer my heart today so that I can be transformed from the inside out. Today I cling to the words found in Psalm 139:23-24, "23 Search me, O God, and know my heart; test me and know my anxious thoughts. 24 Point out anything in me that offends you, and lead me along the path of everlasting life." God, you know my heart, and as I continually seek to please You, I remain open to your conviction, correction, but also your unique calling for my life. Help me to find and live out my personal assignment and to remain confident in your will. I will be set apart today, a willing instrument, ready for your use. In Jesus Name, Amen.

THE CHANGE CHAPTER
CREATING LIFESTYLE CHANGES THAT LAST

Recently I received a notice that my iPhone had an upgrade available. (What else is new!) Initially, I wasn't interested, but after seeing some of the new features and ways the phone was enhanced, I decided to go through with the process. There was only one problem. I didn't have enough space on my phone for the upgrade. So I ended up having to delete apps, messages, and more to create the necessary space for such improvements. Why does this have anything to do with our journey in faith development? Because it is this challenge that takes place in our lives day after day when it comes to effectively making lifestyle changes. When you're purchasing children's shoes, they tell you check to make sure there's "room to grow", when you purchase a child's bed they say to make sure there is "room to grow", when you buy clothes for a child they say, *"Don't get just their present size, because there has to be 'room to grow.'"* See where I'm headed with this? There can be no development where there is no space to grow. When we talk about changes we would like to see in our lives but don't create the space for growth, we stunt the potential of our progress. Real growth requires the substitution of bad habits with good ones, replacing negative influences with positive ones, or tempting environments with supportive settings. In other words, change will always start with a choice. This is an essential step, as one must be willing to go through the process which often involves some level of discomfort and uncertainty. In this chapter, we will explore some practical steps to effect change and how to maintain that change throughout your life. As we dive into this process let me give this disclaimer, this is not the easy part. It is only deep and dedicated commitment that will sustain what you start.

Ready for the ugly truth? Change management is closely related to that of a complicated surgery. It's a season where weak areas are identified, removed or treated for the good of our health. This process is followed by a recovery period, which can often be the most challenging part. And while we know the rewards of such discipline, most people don't give up in the land of their promise. They give up in the land of their present. It's about the discomfort and desperation of now that often call us out of healthy processes. And while all these steps I'm about to mention can be painful, we stay committed knowing we will come out better than before. The truth is some of us would prefer to stay sick to avoid the pain that comes with getting better! Stay focused and allow the process to work through you. Just like good medicine; it can be tough to get down but produces healthy results.

No discipline is enjoyable while it is happening—it's painful! But afterward, there will be a peaceful harvest of right living for those who are trained in this way. Hebrews 12:11 (NLT)

SO HOW DO WE GROW?: IDENTIFICATION

The first step of growth is identification! You must identify what things, what places, or what people currently affect your life the most. We all are "influenced" by something, someone, somewhere, but self-awareness is often the most under-appreciated element of identity in our world. Once identified, you have to assess if these people, places, and things are in alignment with the direction your life is headed. As you read you might be feeling like that doesn't sound like much of a revelation, but for many, this is a daunting task. Most of us are professionals at dealing with symptoms and not sources. People who treat surface symptoms and not the cause of these symptoms often find temporary results, but before long the same patterns reappear in their lives. Identifying areas where change is necessary for growth will take more than a diagnosis, but constant observation. It is the beginning of a deep dive into your being. Once we peek beyond the layers, we create to hide the sources of our own issues we can address the cause of behaviors and attitudes in our lives. However, when one identifies the source of certain thoughts or certain behaviors it puts you in position to move forward with step two of growth, preparation.

PREPARATION

Preparation is a must if you are to be successful in creating space to grow. When I played football (As brief a season that was in my life...lol), I recall the coach challenging us to watch the game film not just of our opponents, but of ourselves. When I inquired as to the "why" of such an activity, he said words I'll never forget, "There is strength in knowing your weaknesses!" In the preparation phase of your process, you must remember two critical things that are essential to your success: honesty and counsel. Truth or Dare? Ok, truth! The most significant battle you'll fight in life won't be against others. It will be against yourself. It's against insecurities, ambitions, fears, failures, bitterness, emptiness, scars from the past, and disappointments of the present. To successfully plan for victory against yourself, you must have the ability to honest with yourself. The person people lie to the most is themselves. Embrace truth and find freedom. For how can one effectively plan when they don't acknowledge the areas in which they have the least control. When we are honest with ourselves, it empowers us to assess where we require new boundaries so that growth can take root in our lives. Truth be told, many of us have a "Mirror, Mirror on the Wall" mentality. We only like looking if it's telling us what we want to hear. But the age-old phrase remains the same. The truth shall set you free.

Additionally, your ability to receive wise counsel is a must during this process. Bouncing difficulties, uncertainties, and fear off of trusted people will often lead to significant dialogue and even better decision making. This is most effective when you establish a covenant group of people you trust, that dare to be honest with you even when it hurts, and can pour wisdom into your life. In a world that pushes us to post a picture of perfection, finding places, where perfection is not a pre-requisite, is crucial to our growth. We all need a circle or a voice we can trust. Once you've received honesty and counsel, put a plan in place to be successful. Former professional runner back Emmitt Smith once said, "All men are created equal, some just work harder in pre-season!" This statement was made after he successfully won his first Super Bowl and was preparing for the challenges of the next season. Your success will be determined not by what problems are thrown at you, but how well you prepare for them in your pre-season. Let's look at this practically: Write down a list of your current challenges and where you most encounter those challenges! (Knowing locations in which you are exposed to your challenges is as important as diagnosing the challenge itself. Environments matter! Exposing open wounds to the wrong environments before they are healed can cause re-infection!) Develop specific goals (Make them clear so you can stay on track!) Make it Visible (Post it on the refrigerator, put a daily reminder on your phone, place it in the front of your most frequently used folder or work bag. Whatever is necessary to remind you daily of growth.)

EXECUTION

Next, and probably the most challenging step in the process, execution. Most people I converse with want to grow, but it's the uncertainty of a new circle, the fear of failure or judgment, or even the inability to step out of comfort zones that cause us to be hindered in our growth. Change is a much-needed part of growth, without it, you fail to evolve into a new season and a new creature. Execution is simply sticking to the plan that you have prepared, and it's all about that "D" word...discipline! Many of us love to live off of miracles and not disciplines; the execution of the latter prevents the constant need for the former. Miracles are designed for rescue. Disciplines are designed for protection! Effective execution is directly connected to this question, "How bad do you want it?" A lot of us say we want to make some healthy changes in our lives, but when it comes to the execution that is necessary, we lack the courage to do whatever it takes. This level of the process is all about surgery; the cutting away, sowing back up and putting things in their proper place. You may have moments where it seems like you're progressing slowly but remember two important things.

CHRISTIANITY IS NOT A COMPETITION

Often we measure our spiritual success by what we observe in others relationship, and when we feel as if we can never do what they do we regress into old habits. But only God knows your experiences, exposures, and efforts, so remember there is no award for best Christian! And that the most amazing part about God is he doesn't look at your outside appearance, he looks at your heart. Which leads to the second thought.

CHRISTIANITY IS NOT ABOUT GETTING TO "A PLACE," BUT ABOUT YOUR CONSISTENT PROGRESS

I am convinced that we often marginalize our spiritual growth because we have a "place" of arrival and not a lifestyle we are pursuing. Fight off the mindset of complacency and make a decision that every day I want to become better at loving God. I'll never arrive at the perfect place in my Christian journey, but I just want to progress every day and be better than the day before. Execution will create a better future and a stronger tomorrow.

EVALUATION

Finally, as one starts executing you must submit yourself to regular evaluation. In every job, every sport, every class there is a method to measure how effectively you are applying the principles introduced to you during that season. The same applies to your growing relationship with God and Christian experience. If you specifically outline your challenges, opportunities for improvement, and goals, it should be easy to evaluate how well you've executed them. Not only should you make these items visible to you, but once you've established a covenant circle find one or two persons to share them with as well. The reality is sometimes we need a push, word of encouragement, check-up call, or a strong word of correction. Depending on your circumstances you may need a different approach but no matter what set up a system of evaluation. God didn't design this journey for you to travel alone, but rather for you to connect with others who have like-minded goals and can walk with you into your new season.

Making lifestyle changes is all about committing to healthier decisions and desiring more positive results spiritually, emotionally, mentally, and socially out of our lives. God's desire for you is to live a great life, full of joy, peace, stability, and prosperity. For many of us as we began to restore our relationship with God and grow in Christian lifestyle changes will be a critical part of us getting into position to claim those qualities of life that are promised to His children. I know you can do it! Don't be afraid of the process and never walk alone!

The Change Devotional

Proverbs 23:7
"For as a man thinketh in his heart, so is he...."

Romans 12:2
"Don't copy the behavior and customs of this world, but let God transform you into a new person by changing the way you think. Then you will learn to know God's will for you, which is good and pleasing and perfect."

When I was first diagnosed with cancer, they informed me of the symptoms of both the sickness and the treatment. It was deflating to think of all the changes my body and life was about to go through. But equally as important, they specified the source of said symptoms, where the tumor was, how far it had spread, and how to remove it and begin the process of restoration. I didn't know it at the time, but this would be the first of many operations, but I remember asking, *"Why are we cutting so much if the cancer is only in one place?"* To which the surgeon graciously replied, *"Because we can't just remove the site of cancer, we also have to clean, cut, and care for the areas that feed the sickness as a preventative measure."* As you prepare to apply change in your life, remember that it's not just about the body, it's about the heart and mind. It's not just about the behavior it's about why we do it. It's not just about the drug. It's about why we feel we can't live without it. And as you think so you'll be. So become. Work inside out to change the way you think, feel and ultimately live. Change is for the taking so claim yours!

Reflection Questions:

What is one area of your life that you'll apply change to this month?

Is this a source or a symptom?

What part of the growth process do you feel will be most challenging for you? (Identification Preparation, Execution, Evaluation)

Inside-Out:

_____

_____

_____

_____

_____

_____

_____

_____

_____

_____

_____

_____

_____

Devotional Prayer

God help me see me in a new way today. I pray for self-awareness and truth to consume my life. I yield to your voice and your process, trusting that the best version of myself has yet to be seen. I start with my heart and mind and pray for transformation from the inside out. Today I walk in freedom. Every struggle and every shackle will fall off of my life, and I will walk incompleteness. I will see your hand at work in my life, and my mind will be renewed and ready for change. I will guard open wounds and invite you in to heal any areas that are not ready to be exposed. Help me to find the joy in discipline and confidence to sustain change. I am a new creation in Christ Jesus, and nothing in the world can take that from me. Thank you, God for the gift of grace. I honor my second chance with the joy of change. In Jesus Name, Amen.

THE PRAYER CHAPTER
THE POWER AND PURPOSE OF PRAYER

In the summer of 2011, I got married to my high school sweetheart. As I anxiously sat in the "holding room" awaiting the start of the ceremony, I reflected on the history of our relationship and recognized how much we had grown over the years. Particularly in the area of communication. I began to think about the conversations of that sixteen-year-old couple, so self-seeking and superficial. Or the college couple that was incredibly inconsistent. Even as I looked at myself, in particular, I was shocked by the immaturity of my expectations that only allowed me to see every situation through the lens of my needs and desires. I was pretty selfish when I took the time to think about it. Wondering why she married me at this point.

Thankfully, I evolved, matured, and grew to understand that some conversations needed to demonstrate more than what benefited me. I learned to communicate my appreciation for what she added to my life. I learned to celebrate her faithfulness and endurance, while other times I discovered the power of confessing truths about motives, actions, or unintentional disappointments. And probably best of all, I learned how to communicate moments when we I fell in love with her all over again, not because of what she did but just because of who she was. If it sounds like I'm writing a book about how to grow in a relationship well, I am! It hit me that our relationship grew in depth because we had learned to express ourselves to each other on multiple levels, thus creating a deeper level of intimacy. God desires this deeper level of intimacy with you! The sad truth is when many of us begin our relationship with God we are only shown "self-seeking" and "surface-level" engagement. In this shallow example, prayer time is the sum of our desires and desperations and not our depth in relationship and dependency on God's presence.

So what's the big deal with prayer? I would like to suggest that prayer is more than what Webster defines as a *"request for help or expression of thanksgiving...,"* But instead it is the very foundation by which your relationship with God grows. If intimacy is the product of emotional access and transparency, a oneness being forged by way of seeing into another, I would argue that prayer is the greatest avenue to growing one with God. In this chapter, we will explore the different forms of prayer, the challenges of having an effective prayer life, and how to kickstart your prayer life.

HOW DO I PRAY?

As a Pastor, there are few moments in my life more entertaining then the face I receive when I ask someone to pray unexpectedly. All too often the phrase I hear is, *"I don't know how to pray!"* This is a common statement made by believers of all ages and stages that is either ineffectively developed or completely ignored as "typical." A huge tragedy because effective prayer is not characterized by powerful language or knowledge of scripture, but rather by one's measure of sincerity. Your story, your trials, your failures, your temptations, your exposures, your desires, your motives, your past, your present, and your potential future all make you qualified to pray. Prayer is simply a conversation with God. Sometimes for others, sometimes for ourselves, but always rooted in authenticity and openness. As you grow in comfort with the act of prayer, you must also consider your approach to prayer. I am a firm believer that there is no "prime position" to pray in. By that I mean some enjoy getting on their knees, others in a sanctuary, for my grandmother she loves a sunrise prayer time (not my testimony), but none of those may be the position in which you feel most comfortable praying. Here's the good news, God doesn't care about your physical position as much as he does your spiritual position. Learn to discipline the mind, heart, and spirit in preparation for God-moments, and then just start talking.

Equally as important to assess is where you feel comfortable praying. Many of us have heard the term "Prayer Closet" and have taken it literally. A prayer closet is literally the space or environment by which you eliminate distractions and interruptions for the purpose of having a purified heart and a listening ear. When possible, it's always great to have a room or place you have set aside to experience God and grow in intimacy intentionally. However, often this is not the case and it is not the only way to experience intimate time with God. Personally, I pray my best prayers in my car. I can recall vividly my mom walking around our house at 5:00 in the morning, praying aloud, just walking in circles over and over again (...as if no one was sleep! But we'll talk about that later!) John Wesley, pioneer of the United Methodist denomination, is quoted as saying his mother would often sit in a chair and put an apron over her head as an indicator to her children to leave her alone. (As a new parent I'm going to give that a shot and see how it works...) The point is, don't ever again be limited to a specific look, sound, or place while praying, but in every prayer seek sincerity and openness! Your life has equipped you with all you need to have a sincere conversation with God!

CHALLENGES TO PRAYING

Liberating as all that may be, there are some challenges we face in developing a healthy and intimate prayer life with God. As I think about these challenges, , the first that comes to mind is a word that I've used several times already this chapter, sincerity. I remember on one occasion speaking with my wife during a time in which I was in the "dog house." I recall preparing an eloquent discourse by which I knew would win her heart over only to be interrupted mid-sentence with these words, "Don't tell me what you think I want to hear, speak from your heart!" I was stuck because while my words were presented with great passion and poise, they lacked the most important ingredient, sincerity.

It is my firm belief that many of us approach our prayer lives with God in the same fashion; great words, passionate presentation but little heart. Sincerity is defined as being free from pretense or deceit; proceeding from genuine feelings. This means my intimacy with God is not just developed by compliments, but by also being true to my feelings, fears, and frustrations. I'd even like to take that a step further by suggesting this truth that I've found in my life. Good prayers don't just make statements but ask questions. Asking God questions when done with the right attitude and with a submissive heart is not a statement lacking faith, but rather an expression of sincerity by which God appreciates. Many feel as if questions have no place in our faith, I believe otherwise. Questions help authenticate our faith. If you've never asked God Who?, What?, When?, Where?, or Why?, you haven't really stepped out of the boat to walk on water, faced your Goliath, or looked at your own Red Sea. Questions have a place in our prayer life, , and the product of prayer should be the fueling of our faith. Faith is not the absence of fear. Rather it's an intersection of influence. An intersection where you either tell your flesh, fears and failures that it can feed your future. Or you remind them that you will be influenced by your "Spirit" and not your "Struggle." This is crucial to understand as we develop intimacy in our prayer life because it empowers us to find comfort in God. When is the last time you told God, *"I felt like you left me alone,"* ? When is the last time you asked God, *"Why did you let me go through this issue or condition?"*? When is the last time you told God, *"I'm confused, and I have no idea what you're doing..."* ? I would like to suggest that it's through these genuine moments of conversation with God that your relationship grows deeper and you're able to connect beyond the surface of church rhetoric and traditional discourse. Let your prayers be a sincere conversation.

Additionally, there is the practical challenge of availability for many people when it comes to their prayer life. In the midst of a culture that says 140 characters is all you get to deliver your message, move as quick as you can, and don't stay in one place too long, we struggle to find time to truly spend with God for intimate conversations. I would like to issue a challenge to every person reading this who says, *"I don't know when I have time to ."* Try these three daily routines to overcome this barrier. First, start your day off with prayer and make God the centerpiece of your morning as opposed to your worries, deadlines, assignments, fatigue, etc. Placing God first helps us invade our humanity with higher thoughts and influence. This invitation for the spirit to work in us and through us each day helps us remain discerning, disciplined, directed throughout our day. How do you do this you ask? Ideally, I'd say wake up a little early, even if only 10-15 minutes, and take the time to pray before you get up and moving. However, I know that some of us ALWAYS hit the snooze button at least three times, wait to the very last minute to roll out of bed and get out the door with just enough time to make it to our destination. If this is you, and waking up a little early is not an option that you feel you can be consistent with, I suggest what I call the "Substitution Method." Substitute your morning music with silence in the car and prayer, just those 10-20 minutes it takes to get to work, school, or wherever you may be going will start your day off making God the priority.

Maybe you walk? Instead of a phone call just spend some time praying while you trek from place to place. Now I know what some of you are saying, "I'm going to look crazy talking to myself walking down the street!" , and I'm inclined to say looking crazy is ok. But there is a healthy compromise, and it's what we call "breath prayers." These prayers are characterized by focusing on specific thoughts or meditations while mumbling quietly to yourself as you spend time with God. This is also another effective way to get prayers in at any time throughout your day, no matter your location. Third, and probably one of the most underutilized tools in developing a prayer life, WRITE IT DOWN ON PAPER! You can write a prayer for the week or the month and just read it aloud at some point during your day as a declaration over your life. An example of this would be:

Today I will strive to represent Christ in all that I do! I will work my hardest to make sure my attitude, conversations, work ethic, actions, and reactions reflect my growing relationship with God. I know that I belong to God and that every day is a new opportunity to draw closer to him. Protect me God from dangers seen and unseen, physically, emotionally, mentally, and spiritually! I will do all that I can to make today my best day! Amen!

This is a simple and quick way to develop consistency in your prayer life. You can write your own or find one, but no matter what, remember sincerity is the key! Several have been provided for you throughout this book that can be used whenever needed. Lastly, I challenge you to make time at some point in your day for not only talking to God but listening to God. Even if its ten minutes, make that ten minutes time where your phone goes off, you go to a focused place and allow yourself to meditate or center your thoughts. God doesn't always speak audibly, but sometimes in these moments, he speaks through clarifying things or enabling you to finally get that idea that you've been waiting for. He also convicts you about decisions you've made and can challenge you to set new standards in your life. Prayer time is not only time to talk, but time to listen and to be molded by God's spirit. Take the time to let God speak to your heart. You'll be surprised what five focused minutes can do!

FORMS OF PRAYER

Finally, we must explore the different forms of prayer. A one-dimensional relationship can't survive, and so it is that your prayer life must be diverse enough to reflect the depth of your spiritual relationship. As one looks at the different forms of prayer, you hopefully can see how these various elements can build intimacy and power. So let's look at the five forms of prayer.

Adoration: Prayer that reflects deep love or esteem for God. This form of prayer should be incorporated into our everyday life as it enables you to tell God what you love about him! These moments are filled with what amazes you about God. The beauty of nature, an appreciation for how the sun sets and the moon rises at just the right time, the intricacies of a caterpillar crawling until it's time of transformation into a beautiful butterfly, the stars set upon the dark backdrop of the sky. Or you could take moments to notice and name the beauty of people you observe. The man helping a senior woman across the street, the mother carrying new life and the innocence of the child's eyes, the joy when you see real love on display or the peace of a life lived on purpose. Noticing God's heart, hands at work, peace, and power all around you is a powerful way to adore God. Adoration prayers encourage us to take time out to admire God and remind yourself just why you love him!

Intercession: Prayer that is done on behalf of someone or something else. This form of prayer occurs when you take a moment out to recognize the needs of someone else. In a world that constantly encourages selfish ambition and attention, intercession challenges us to focus on the needs of others in our lives; petitioning God on their behalf instead of our own. These moments could also be comprised of prayer for larger cultural or national issues, and lifting up these concerns to God in confidence that his hand can reach beyond your locality into lands you may not live in. Intercession challenges us to pray for needs that do not benefit us personally.

Supplication: Also known as a "Prayer of Petition." This form of prayer asks God to supply wants and needs. Arguably the most common prayer there is because of its beneficial nature, these moments are full of our personal needs, desires, and expectations. We go to God with confidence and clarity, knowing that what we come seeking is not greater than God's capacity. Supplication is the prayer that makes known to God our "ask" and requests his action on our behalf. Thanksgiving: Prayer that takes time out to thank God for ways in which he's provided previously or presently. These prayers don't always have to reflect major needs being met, but can also represent daily blessings such as life, health, and family. They can also be very reflective, as we bask in memories and testimony of how God has consistently provided and protected in our lives. Thanksgiving should be a language we speak in more than November, but throughout our year so we can effectively celebrate God's consistency.

Repentance: Prayer that asks God for forgiveness. This form of prayer should be coupled with a desire to make necessary life changes and with intentions to alter the identified action or activity. No one is perfect, which is why there will always be a need for repentance. But one must also evaluate their heart to determine if they truly desire to change their behavior, or are they just telling God what they think he wants to hear. Such prayers lack sincerity. This does not mean they shouldn't pray, but that the request should be made for the desire to be removed or to be truthful with God about where you stand in that particular struggle. We should always come to God knowing grace is available, and that his perfect sacrifice makes it possible for us to be made new, washed clean, and redeemed.

All in all, prayer is the key by which intimacy with God is unlocked. As you start to develop your prayer life your love life will grow, your desires will change to those that more closely reflect your relationship with God, and you will begin to see a deeper passion birthed for something more than religion, but a relationship. Remember God wants more than cliches and compliments, but he desires to have a sincere conversation with you every day so that you may grow with him in true love!

The Prayer Devotional

Philippians 4:6
6 Don't worry about anything; instead, pray about everything. Tell God what you need, and thank him for all he has done. 7 Then you will experience God's peace, which exceeds anything we can understand. His peace will guard your hearts and minds as you live in Christ Jesus.

Communication is essential to the growth of any relationship. For any of us who've ever been in any relationship of significance, we can testify to this reality. When we are open and consistent, it opens up understanding, confidence, and unity in unimaginable ways. It's this level of oneness that we seek with people we love. How much more should we seek it with God? Have you ever been in a relationship with someone who was open or failed to be truthful? It damages that level of intimacy you can reach when the conversation is inconsistent or insincere. Prayer is the single most important way to both start and sustain intimacy with God. Make it apart of your daily life as a discipline. Don't be afraid to be yourself and remember; there's more than one way to pray.

Reflection Questions:

Which area of your prayer life is most utilized based on the five areas highlighted in the chapter?

Which area of your prayer life is least activated at this time? What will you do to strengthen this area?

Listening is equally as important as speaking in our prayer time. How will you make time to listen to God's voice this week?

Inside-Out:

_____
_____
_____
_____
_____
_____
_____
_____
_____
_____
_____
_____
_____
_____

Devotional Prayer

Today I release worry and cling to confidence in your promises. Your word tells me that your word never fails and that greater is he within me than he that is within the world. So because I trust your word, I can walk in peace. Not because the problem is resolved, but because I know in your hands it's already taken care of. Help me to rest in your plan and process. I claim protection over my heart and mind and peace that surpasses all understanding. In Jesus Name, Amen.

Prayer Pledge

Lord, I want to know you more. I want to move beyond the surface and find deeper levels of our relationship. I commit to always be honest, open, and sincere in our time together. I also commit to listening, so that I can receive what you might speak to my ears, my heart, or my mind. I will make time with you the greatest priority of my life. I place you at the center of my world. Every Day!

THE BIBLE CHAPTER
HOW TO READ THE BIBLE

In May of 2013, I began working out heavily with a trainer to transform my body. He made it very clear that he sought to develop me not only physically, but also nutritionally. This is the fundamental message of great health and fitness because a body that you work out but feed improperly will produce limited results. What an amazing concept of creation? You can be in a place with everything you need to grow, but you have to consume the right things to produce evidence of your transformation. This is what I suggest is at the core of reading the Bible within the Christian faith. Having religious activity, a church service, a ministry to volunteer on are all are great ways to "workout" or "exercise" your faith, but when you leave that moment, what are you consuming to produce sustainable growth?

Have you ever made up in your mind that you were going to read the Bible, and shortly after that asked yourself, *"Where do I start?"*. Or how about opened it up only to find your eyelids shutting, head nodding, and eventually sleep was knocking on your door? These are very common problems for people on all spiritual levels, as reading the Bible is no "one-size-fits-all-task"! This God-inspired work we call the Bible is full of miraculous stories, relevant wisdom, life-changing quotes, and transformative guidance. No wonder it's been the best selling book for hundreds of years. However, we often lose interest in reading because we struggle to find these golden nuggets buried beneath ancient language, cultural context, and historical rhetoric. In this chapter we will explore some practical solutions to Bible reading by addressing three key questions; How do I read the Bible? What should I read first? And when should I read the Bible?

WHEN DO I READ?

Knowing that you're eager to jump in and dust off that high-school graduation gift from Grandma let me caution you really quick to wait one moment. I don't want to discourage your enthusiasm to begin reading, but I'd like to equip you with this small piece of preparation that changed my life. While the act of reading the Bible is important, there is also an art to reading as well, and it starts with self-awareness. More specifically, knowing when to read is a critical element of effective study that we often overlook in our teaching. Remember, this undertaking is no "one-size-fits-all-task," so assessing the time when your mind is most capable of learning is crucial. Reading the Bible is one thing; reading, reflecting, wrestling, taking notes, and eventual internalization and application is an entirely different experience that takes mental commitment and intentionality. Now before I scare you to throw that Bible back in the corner fear not, I've got you covered.

I remember being in my Sophomore year of college and my grades were falling. (Falling sounds so much better than failing doesn't it? I digress!) I had a desire to learn, but I could not seem to stay focused or committed to the assignments in front of me; I constantly fell asleep on night-time work and going to the library felt more like going to a weekday party. Halfway through the semester, I realized something had to change, or my parents were going to change my residence back to my home address. I found through honest self-evaluation that I could not focus my best at night due to the various options vying for my attention. Additionally, I discovered that it was easier for me to read and retain in a small study group, even if they were reading different things, opposed to a larger group where many alternative conversations could arise. Lastly, I found that my thoughts were most centered early in the morning when there were limited social distractions. Even as I write this chapter it's 4:56 am, no texts are buzzing on my phone, no kids screaming *"Daddy!"*, and no distractions in sight. With all that in mind, I began a new study pattern which included waking up a couple of hours before everyone else to complete assignments. I found that I had limited distractions, fresh energy, and maximum results. I believe the same practicality of preparation is necessary to the reading of your Bible. The question only you can answer is, when will I receive this information the best? Keeping in mind that the goal is not only to see the word, but retain the word, and grow from the word of life. Here are some questions you can ask yourself to help you best achieve this goal:

When am I most energized? (Some of us are morning people, and others are not, finding out when your energy is at is peak is a great resource.)

When am I most focused? (What time of the day can I give quality attention to the task?)

Where am I most focused? (For some of us reading in our bed is a "death-wish" an impossible task, but for others, it can be therapeutic.)

What group of people have a similar interest as me? (Finding study partners and people to bounce ideas and discussions off of is a great catalyst to study further. Pick a topic of the week, , and each of you find scriptures that relate or speak to you personally and share with the group. This not only sparks conversation but exposes you to more than just your findings; remember, it's a big book!)

Finding out when and where to read is a critical step in developing healthy study habits and seeing growth. Remember, this is the stuff that will produce the transformative results you desire. Being an active believer is great, but what you put in your mind, heart, and spirit matter equally as much so that what has been started can be sustained.

WHAT DO I READ?

Believing that I didn't scare you off in the first section by asking you to "take notes," it's time to crack open that study Bible now. I can tell you, once I decided to commit to reading the bible I remember saying, *"This is a really big book, where in the world do I start?"* And for those like me who thought to start in Genesis and read straight through Revelation was a good idea quickly found out how lost in "The Word" we could be. So here's my personal philosophy on reading the Bible and it's simple. Don't go to the Bible, bring the Bible to you!" Now depending on the maturity and longevity of your faith walk, maybe it's time for you to study specific topics, themes, or text that God has revealed to you are necessary for your continual growth. But for those who are trying to develop both interest and consistency, it is my firm belief that you'll waiver as long as you blindly read passages trying to understand a world that we have never encountered, people we will never meet, and a culture that is long gone in many ways. However, "bringing the Bible to you" is all about assessing your current needs, curiosities, and context. I then encourage finding passages that connect to your context and curiosities, ultimately bridging the gap of relevancy as the Bible has now met you in a place you never thought it could.

I know what you're saying, so how do I find these relevant passages? Sounds too good to be true! Here are a few practical recommendations and the first is probably the deepest. Here it is, are you ready? Wait for it...Search Engines. *insert dramatic face or side eye here* While this may seem extremely trivial and maybe even carnal, Google is one of the most valuable resources available to us as people of faith. When we're looking up information on the latest gossip in the entertainment industry we go to search engines, the latest stats for sports, search engines, the "How to" questions, search engines, yet when it comes to growing in biblical understanding we limit ourselves to traditional forms of content exploration. It's a really big book, and it's easy to get loss flipping through pages without the pages ever flipping you. Now let me be clear if there is someone in your life who can help guide you through this process of foundational biblical studies, take full advantage of that resource. A minister or knowledgeable friend is invaluable when you are starting to read and understand the Bible. However, there are times we don't have access to "one-on-one" sessions to walk us through reading the Bible effectively. So when you are alone or away from those persons, I believe this can be of great service, as we can make any place "HOLY" with the spirit and attitude we bring to it! So start with an interest, curiosity, or need, and look for scriptures that relate to that experience. Let's look at a couple examples of how this works: (*actual searches performed by our team)

PRACTICE:

Need/Interest: *How do I keep my faith in difficult times?*
Search: *"Scriptures about Faith."*

Results: *Philippians 4:6-7*
"6 Don't worry about anything; instead, pray about everything. Tell God what you need, and thank him for all he has done. 7 Then you will experience God's peace, which exceeds anything we can understand. His peace will guard your hearts and minds as you live in Christ Jesus."

James 1:2-4
"Dear brothers, is your life full of difficulties and temptations? Then be happy, for when the way is rough, your patience has a chance to grow. So let it grow, and don't try to squirm out of your problems. For when your patience is finally in full bloom, then you will be ready for anything; strong in character, full and complete."

These are two very different passages that could be encouraging when enduring a situation in which one lacks faith. To internalize the message of these passages, and embrace that my life may be full of difficulty right now, but this is apart of a process and can be a catalyst to my growth may just give the push we need to make it through the week. Or to see that once we pray we should let it go and allow God's peace to overtake us. And it is that peace that guards our heart, our mind, and all of our being! In addition to these scriptures, one could also look up "biblical stories about faith" and find a wealth of characters and situations that may parallel with one's current context. Additionally, two other forms of technology could be of great benefit to rejuvenating Bible reading passion. The first is the "Bible Project," which takes biblical content and produces visual storytelling to bring each story to life. A powerful tool for both engagement and understanding. And of course, the "Bible App," which is full of features like reminders, prepared plans, and note taking ability that can help develop your devotional life.

There are many versions of the Bible app at this point, and while I won't advocate for a specific one, I'd recommend downloading one for the accessibility and accountability it can provide. In addition to utilizing technology as an ally and not an enemy, I also strongly suggests readings that strengthen the core of your faith and give you practical advice on being a fruit-bearing believer. THIS IS A MUST DO AS A BELIEVER!

Here are my top three suggestions on where to start reading:

Read about Jesus: THE GOSPELS (Matthew, Mark, Luke, & John tell us all about Jesus and his work on earth.) These books chronicle the life of Jesus and show us his example of "Christian" living. They also point us back to the source of our faith and remind us that our life is the product of the ultimate sacrifice, Jesus death, burial, and resurrection. This life gave us life, and that's the GOOD NEWS.

Proverbs: (Great words of wisdom and practical in presentation. Generally 2-4 verses at a time is more comfortable for one to digest and apply. I consider them "bite-sized" empowerment)

James: (a Great book that outlines how "Christians" should carry themselves in conversation, behavior, and attitude. I find this book to be a bold mirror, challenging us to look at ourselves frequently and see the good, bad and ugly, in order to produce positive change.)

HOW DO I READ?

Having a starting point is great, but understanding "how to read" this amazing book can be challenging as well. With so many cultural dynamics screaming off the pages, ancient language, and even political undertones, it is easy to misinterpret or all-together lack understanding of a particular passage of scripture. I encourage readers to employ three phases to your reading; Translation, Meditation, and Application. Initially, we find a passage of scripture that meets our need, and we read the first translation that becomes available to us; STOP RIGHT THERE! Different translations can give you a very personal appeal that otherwise would be absent, connecting you to a passage beyond what you could ever imagine. Even as a minister I read certain passages and ask myself, *"What in the world are they talking about?"* This is the frustration of many who are new readers. This tragedy can be avoided as technology, and other advancements have made accessibility to different translations as simple as the click of a button. That is not to say that the easiest to understand translation is always the most accurate. But I believe what's most important is understanding and consistency. Read multiple translations and find clarity.

Next, we must take time to meditate on scriptures that meet our need. Meaning, time must be taken to engage the passage in such a way that God can speak to you personally. For example, as I recently mentioned I set out on a quest to get in shape some time ago. As I sat with my workout partner at lunch one day I began to eat as I normally do, very quickly. He advised me to eat slower, suggesting that anatomically my body would then be able to process the amount I'm eating and I would become full faster, as opposed to moving on to the next meal so quickly. The same applies to getting "full" off of scripture! Once you find a passage that meets your need chew on it for a while and don't be so eager to move on. Allow it to "fill" you and become apart of you. It is when you take different texts piece by piece and really sit with them that you'll see it manifest in your lifestyle the most. The goal is definitely not quantity. It's quality.

Lastly, always ask the question, "How does this apply to my life?" Application matters! Often we can quote scriptures but struggle to apply them to our life. In this step of understanding "how to read," take each passage or story and say, *"How will I use this tomorrow, and the day after that?"* If disciplined enough, even set challenges for yourself to try and apply the information found at least once or twice in your day as you learn how to really allow the words you read to "order your steps."

BE PATIENT

Please understand, this is a lifetime commitment and never a race. Also, let me reiterate that there is no substitute for a ministry leader or knowledgeable person as a guide throughout this journey. Being apart of a regular Bible study or spiritual development group helps you gain consistent access to new information and insight as you progress in your understanding and hunger. In a Bible that is "so big," this approach places you in the neighborhood of scriptures that relate to your interest. This is just a start. Once you get rolling, you'll find different resources that will introduce you to a whole new world of readings, commentaries, and ways to grow spiritually through the word. But just start, and know if you open it enough, it will start to change you in ways you've never imagined.

The Bible Devotional

Hebrews 4:12
"For the word of God is alive and powerful. It is sharper than the sharpest two-edged sword, cutting between soul and spirit, between joint and marrow. It exposes our innermost thoughts and desires."

I'm sure we've all heard the phrase before "Sticks and Stones may break my bones but words will never hurt me." Since when? I can only speak for myself but in my experience words hurt, words heal, words have power, words discourage, words develop, words matter. This is why keeping our words rooted in "The Word" is so important. God's inspired word has the power to change our lives from the inside out. May we all find new found joy and curiosity in the exploration of God's word. I promise you, in his word you'll find what you need for every season.

Reflection Questions:

What is the greatest challenge to your biblical commitment?

How do you plan to overcome this?

Who is a biblical character that connects with you on a personal level?

Is there any technology that could support the growth of your bible study?

Inside-Out:

_____

_____

_____

_____

_____

_____

_____

_____

_____

_____

_____

_____

Devotional Prayer

This is the day the Lord has made. I will rejoice and be glad in it. Today I commit to finding joy in every moment. I stand in great expectation of my future. But I also walk in excitement for my present. My commitment to myself is to smile religiously, share freely, and speak boldly about my faith and how it has changed my life. This day is a gift, and I cherish it by living well today. In Jesus Name, Amen.

THE GIVING CHAPTER
DEVELOPING A GENEROUS HEART

There have been many moments that I'm proud of in life, but by far one of the most amazing moments was becoming a parent. I won't bore you with all the cliches that parents say about the birth and beauty of their child, but my children captured my heart and affection immediately. However, what most won't say is after that "googly-eyed" phase comes another season. One that can only be described as a "joyful inconvenience," and that my friends are parenting. This wonderful new world full of new priorities, new perspectives, and a new type of pressure has been a learning experience, to say the least. Not a pressure to perform at work or to produce a momentary result, but to literally produce from scratch an ideal citizen and well-developed human being through both life example and intentional instruction for years to come. This pressure is probably most evident in one of the first lessons we've had to teach our children as we've encountered other families. I mean you don't know pressure until your kid steals another kids toy and refuses to give it back and then pushes them off of the ride because they don't want to wait their turn and screams out "Mine" over and over again and that child starts crying and now their parents are looking at you like what kind of monster are you raising and you look back like I'm sorry I don't know what to say and all the while you're looking at your wife, and she's looking at you like do something, and you don't know what to do, and the embarrassment creeps up on you that you might just be a horrible parent and so you leave abruptly because it's safer that way. (That was an intentional run-on sentence to reflect the actual thoughts that run through parent's head when their child is out of control in public. I will now return to proper grammar at this time.)

As I was saying, all parents teach their child this one central lesson very early in life, sharing! I mean think about it! They can't say full sentences, maybe a few words, and we're already saying to them "Give Me Some." Showing them how to see the world as bigger than their existence and we began to shape the identity of a giver through one simple word, SHARE! Giving in the kingdom is very similar. In a culture full of "selfies," it's hard to see people share much anymore. We are a very "me" focused culture; like "MY" picture, follow "ME," what do "I" get if "I" do that? This type of cultural reality threatens the existence of giving on every level. One of the most amazing things about God is that he "gave" to us first, and we can see it in one of the most popular passages in the Bible, John 3:16 which reads:

16 "For this is how God loved the world: He gave his one and only Son so that everyone who believes in him will not perish but have eternal life. (NLT)

With no identifiable benefit, God gave. And the only prerequisite for his sharing with us was his love. It's love for others that prompts the believer to "share." No benefits needed, no credit, no celebration, just love for all people. Jesus even went on to say the greatest commandment was to "Love your neighbor as you love yourself"! And it's this reality that should drive us as believers to be givers of our time, tithe, and talent to the kingdom. I think God is holding out his hand saying to his children "Give Me Some," let's see how we should respond.

GIVING YOUR TIME

Steve Jobs once said, *"My favorite things in life don't cost any money. It's really clear that the most precious resource we all have is time."* As discussed in earlier chapters, lifestyle changes are the product of great intentionality. I've often told people that I can tell them what they love most if they showed me their schedule. It's in the places that we choose to give our time that we find our true reward and fulfillment. For those who love going to the gym, they feel "off-center" if they miss a few days. Some love running and would feel completely out of sync if they had missed the opportunity for several days. Outside of fitness, some of us truly enjoy quiet time and reading, while others absolutely need to be around people every chance they get. We all find escape and joy in investing our time different ways. But let us never forget time is just that, an investment. And how you choose to invest your time also will determine the type of return you will receive. Interestingly enough, I find that most believers are incentivized to walk with God because of where they want their time to be spent "afterlife", but not for how they will spend their time with "with their life." Every lifestyle change should result in a time change. When people change to a healthier life, they invest more of their time in the gym. When people change their relationship status, they invest more time into getting to know another individual. When people go back to school, they change to an academic lifestyle and invest less time socializing. Likewise, when we commit our lives to experiencing our relationship with God, our time investment should change. Now I know what you're thinking, this is the part where I talk about the importance of church service and how we should spend more time in our Bibles. And while I have affirmed those things in other chapters and their importance to the life of a believer, it is imperative to understand that more church doesn't mean more Christian. That while fellowship is important, it is of the utmost importance that we create time to serve others and display our faith in tangible ways outside of the church.

I've never liked jewelry! I didn't get a class ring in high school, wasn't big on necklaces or chains when that was popular, and never cared much for watches. So naturally, when I got married the wedding ring bothered me a great deal to have on all the time. I know I just lost a majority of my female readers but stay with me for a little while longer. I found that it became easier to remove my ring in private and to return it to my finger when going out in public. Of course, this was a great plan until one day I forgot the ring at home one day. My friend, concerned this could create grave danger asked, *"Do you want to go back and get it? If you don't people won't know you're married."* To which I responded, *"It's not the ring alone that tells people I'm married, it's also my behavior."* Needless to say, I tried to avoid that from ever happening again. But as believers, people should be able to identify our status not by our words, or titles, or apparel, but by our interaction. Check out these words written in James 2:14-22: *"14 What good is it, dear brothers and sisters if you say you have faith but don't show it by your actions? Can that kind of faith save anyone? 15 Suppose you see a brother or sister who has no food or clothing, 16 and you say, "Good-bye and have a good day; stay warm and eat well"—but then you don't give that person any food or clothing. What good does that do? 17 So you see, faith by itself isn't enough. Unless it produces good deeds, it is dead and useless. 18 Now someone may argue, "Some people have faith; others have good deeds." But I say, "How can you show me your faith if you don't have good deeds? I will show you my faith by my good deeds." 19 You say you have faith, for you believe that there is one God.[f] Good for you! Even the demons believe this, and they tremble in terror. 20 How foolish! Can't you see that faith without good deeds is useless? 21 Don't you remember that our ancestor Abraham was shown to be right with God by his actions when he offered his son Isaac on the altar? 22 You see, his faith and his actions worked together. His actions made his faith complete."*

This passage is always a great reminder of our responsibility to others, not ourselves. You might have heard it more commonly stated in another translation, "Faith without works is dead." I believe we've often taken this passage out of context and we've done what we do well in our culture, made it about "us." If we work hard with our faith, this is what we'll get. However, this passage challenges us to do something very different. It pushes us to look beyond ourselves and give of our time in a way that impacts the lives of others. It reminds us that our actions and how we invest our time are what makes our faith complete. Great Christians don't just lift their hands on Sunday, they use their hands throughout the week, to serve others publicly and privately who have a need. We must always remember that the DNA of the Christian is serving others.

GIVING YOUR TITHE

"TEN PERCENT! Do you know what I could do with ten percent of my income?" This was the highlight of a conversation I had recently with one of my friends who was newly introduced to the church. They had recently relocated and determined it was time to see what this "church thing" was all about. After an initial visit, they didn't leave with answers. They left with more questions. Particularly, why should I give all this money to the church? With so much negativity surrounding the management of funds in the church over the last decade, most people have a growing skepticism about where they should invest their money, and the church is not a high priority. Now I'm a pastor so I could write an entire book on the importance of giving with a myriad of scriptures and hermeneutical revelations, but that's not what this book is for. This book is to help you realize why we give at all and then I'd encourage you to more guidance on how you can further your understanding of biblical based giving at a deeper level. Three principles should motivate our giving that I'd like to share.

51

WE DON'T GIVE TO A CHURCH, WE GIVE TO A CAUSE

You've heard me say in a previous chapter that the original word for "church" never referenced a building but rather an assembly of like-minded people all gathered for one cause, kingdom advancement. We all have our own bills, debt, and responsibilities, so naturally giving to support building maintenance is not inspiring. However, if I told you to give towards the restoration of homes in our community, or maybe the college education of a young person who can't afford it, I'd hope you find motivation in seeing that life impacted. Finding a church home is about finding a vision that you believe in. Until you find this home, you will forever struggle with releasing your hard earned resources because you don't believe in the assignment of the people. This is by no means to suggest that cause-driven giving should exclusively be our motivation. Many who'll read this might think I should have started with how we give to God because he deserves it and he first gave to us. But in my experience, I've found that giving usually never starts there for most believers. It starts with our inspiration and support of what the church is doing not just what the church is. *21 Wherever your treasure is, there the desires of your heart will also be. Matthew 6:21 (NLT)*

Your heart will determine where your money goes. If you believe in it, then you'll give to it. If you believe in the iPhone than you will invest in buying each one they release because you know this is worth my investment. Giving must start with your heart. As you start giving to a local church, ask yourself do I believe in what I'm giving to? If you don't, maybe you should schedule a conversation with a leader and ask some questions that will help you discern and develop your enthusiasm and heart for the house.

NEVER GET STUCK ON "10"

Most of us have lived and died by the concept of giving ten percent. So much so that we are bound to this percentage as both the minimum and the maximum of our investment. It is imperative to understand a few things about the ten percent we so comfortably reference in the church. In the Jewish tradition, the tithe was used as a teaching tool for children to help them in understanding giving and stewardship. Similar to when you give a child $50 for chores but tell them they have to put $5 in the offering plate, it's role is to aid us in the discipline of our resources and heart for the kingdom. The problem is many of us are told to be "cheerful" givers but we feel like we're disappointing God when we don't give ten percent. As you read this section, please remember that this book is called *'In the Beginning,'* And is written to help you understand the big "Why" in major faith categories. This book is to hopefully help you understand why we give and what can create healthy considerations for you as you start giving to a local assembly. Considerations I believe will help you not just start giving, but sustain your passion for giving.

Let me be clear, giving is not about how much you give, but developing the habit and lifestyle of kingdom stewardship. That's the power of the percent. It's the same piece for everyone. Whether you make six figures or sixty thousand, it's the same piece. There's a story of a woman in the Bible that affirms this principle of sacrifice being the heart of giving and not the amount.

Mark 12:41-44 Sitting across from the offering box, he was observing how the crowd tossed money in for the collection. Many of the rich were making large contributions. One poor widow came up and put in two small coins—a measly two cents. Jesus called his disciples over and said, "The truth is that this poor widow gave more to the collection than all the others put together. All the others gave what they'll never miss; she gave extravagantly what she couldn't afford—she gave her all."

She gave her all. And God honors the heart that gives it all. While I affirm that God makes very clear biblically that the 10% is set apart and holy, and belongs to the storehouse, I just want you to get started. That may not be ten percent in the beginning, but set a percentage and practice the discipline of giving that amount every month. Whether that's ten percent, eight percent, or four percent, give it every month. But you can't stop there because just like any relationship your success isn't measured by where you started, but how you've grown. Eventually, you could be giving far more than ten percent each month. Because it's not about getting stuck on "ten," it's about the discipline of giving and making kingdom causes a priority in your resources.

NEVER GIVE AS IF YOU OWN

I'm pretty confident we all have had a moment where we loaned something to someone, only for them to act as if they owned it. This became painfully obvious to me during my college years when I loaned a pair of shoes to a friend of mine. Months went by before I ever asked for the shoes back but when I needed them, he gave them to me as if he owned them. Giving me a timeline on when he needed them back again and returning them in a condition that was dismal. This is how we often treat the resources of our lives. How quickly we can forget that every opportunity, financial gain, and favorable moment was a product not only of our hard work but of divine blessing from God. When we truly see all that we have as a result of all that God has given, it changes the heart in which we give from. We no longer find restraint in giving because we recognize we don't own any of it, we've just been favored to possess it and steward it.

While it's important to recognize God owns all that we have, It's also imperative to see mentally, the benefit of this approach. Many people struggle with giving because they see it only as a subtraction in their net income, not as a seed planted into good soil that will grow. You'll never see the joy in giving if it always feels like a "RISK" and not a "RELEASE." Release what you have back to God in trust, and he'll not only honor the sacrifice, but I believe he'll return and reward your faithfulness. And make no mistake about it, Giving is a test. When the Lord asks us in the book of Malachi, *"Will a man/woman rob God?"*, He's talking specifically about the withholding of the tithe. Yes, God takes the tithe so serious that it's like robbing God when we don't give our ten percent. But I love what he goes on to say, *"Test me in this, and see won't I pour out a blessing you don't have room enough to receive."* Tithing is a test; a test of discipline for us and a test of the heart. But it's also the only place in the Bible where God tells us we can test him. So I encourage you today, pass the test, give the test, and sow the tithe.

GIVING YOUR TALENT

Finally, I want to dispel a myth about serving in ministry. Through the years have established that ministry happens far beyond the walls of a church building, and we can safely conclude that we need more than ushers, deacons, praise and worship leaders, and sound engineers to fulfill our kingdom obligation. Beyond the comfort of our Sunday services are the desperate cries for builders, financial advisors, counselors, educators, and social service workers. Those who will worship God through their vocations and commit themselves spiritually to a work that is not compartmentalized to one day a week. It is in understanding that my everyday life is an opportunity to honor God through my purpose and passions that we find true joy and excitement in a Christian journey.

Equally as important is that we bring our gifts to the church. Serving our local church shouldn't be based on benefits or compensation, but rather on how we can honor God with which he has given us. That is not to say we should not honor hard work, ability, and competency through compensation. But when the return becomes the primary motivation of those who serve in our church we lose the authenticity of our worship. When we learn to use our talents to communicate vertically and not horizontally, that's when we will truly experience the fullness of our Christianity. It's not about people or popularity, but using our gifts to show God our appreciation by way of service and excellence. I promise you; there is no greater fulfillment than that of one who brings together their organic passions and talents with their spirituality in such a way that their entire being is a form of worship. Take the talent, and give it back!

The Giving Devotional

Matthew 6:21
21 Wherever your treasure is, there the desires of your heart will also be.

2 Corinthians 9:7
7 You must each decide in your heart how much to give. And don't give reluctantly or in response to pressure. "For God loves a person who gives cheerfully."

What is photosynthesis? Here's my attempt to answer in plain english for my own benefit. Sunlight is received by plants which is a complex process convert light to energy and combine it with carbon dioxide to create food for the plant. The byproduct is the release of oxygen into the Earth which Humanity can't live without. And that my friends, is giving in a nutshell. And here we thought that all that stuff we learned in Biology class would never be useful. In my opinion, to stretch your giving capacity is similar to the plant's process. We receive freely, and we convert a portion of that which we are given into a powerful tool to make the earth a better place. The plant receives freely, and returns generously, a portion to bring life to the world. We receive freely, and should return cheerfully, a portion of that gift to bring life to the world we live in. Sometimes that will be financial, other times with our time or talent. But the gift of life we all possess should result in us giving something back to our world.

Reflection Questions:

What level of giving would you consider yourself to be regularly? (First Time, Emotional, Faithful, Sacrificial, Radical)

How could you improve your stewardship of time, treasure, or talent?

Think about a time that you gave of yourself, and it produced joy in your life. Make that memory your motivation.

Inside-Out:

_____
_____
_____
_____
_____
_____
_____
_____
_____
_____
_____
_____
_____
_____

Devotional Prayer

God all that I am is because of you. All that I have is because of you. All that I am becoming is because of you. I am grateful today for every blessing you've brought into my life. I don't deserve it, but you are faithful in your love and giving to me. So today I commit to releasing my time, my tithe, and my talents for your kingdom. I want to invest my treasure in good ground, and see the way it can change the lives of people in my community and world. I am more than a consumer. I am a contributor. God use my seed today to bring life to someone in need. To bring hope to someone hurting. To bring life to dry bones. In Jesus Name, Amen.

THE FASTING CHAPTER
DEVELOPING THE HEART AND HABIT OF FASTING

We all have done it; the first date! Nerves trembling, mind racing, running through outfit after outfit trying to find the right ensemble. But maybe the most important element (and most difficult) to a great date in the twenty-first century has little to do with what you wear or where you go. But I'd like to suggest it's probably the challenge of not allowing your phone to compete with your attention. Silence your phone! A simple gesture that assures someone they have your undivided attention. A temporary sacrifice that shows personal investment and prioritization. The act of fasting seeks to fulfill a similar purpose. It is a temporary sacrifice of food or drinks with the intention of spending intimate and purposeful time with God. When fasting, one is dedicated to creating intimate time with God with the desire to hear God, seek God, and to develop closeness with God. Fasting is also coupled with the excessing of "disciplines," which are a momentary sacrifice as well, but simply put involves the sacrifice of things other than food or drink. Let's be clear, biblical based fasting specifically references the sacrifice of food or drinks. While disciplines are exemplified by actions such as eliminating social networks for a period or limiting the time you watch television, generally resulting in a mental and social challenge. Fasting and disciplines are two principles that push us into a closer relationship with God but also give us opportunities to "think purely." In this chapter, we'll explore the function of fasting and disciplines, types of fasting, healthy fasting principles, and ways to stay motivated during these periods.

FUNCTION OF FASTING/DISCIPLINES

As stated earlier, fasting by definition is considered abstaining from all or some kinds of food or drink. When trying to conceptualize this activity, I like to think it's most clearly defined by two words, sacrifice, and substitution. The sacrifice, historically defined by food or drink, must be done with honest self-evaluation. The sacrifice of something that is not appetizing to the individual is not a sacrifice at all. If you rarely eat breakfast, letting go of bacon and eggs wouldn't constitute as sacrificial. When evaluating what you will fast from, select something that you'll miss, that you eat or drink weekly or daily for that matter, something that you will notice and feel in your normal routine. Supporting this sacrifice is the act of substitution. Fasting without substitution is simply a glorified diet! Your sacrifice must also be substituted with time dedicated to prayer and pure thoughts. Whether its during the lunch break you normally take, or during the time you'd be preparing dinner, the way to effectively grow from a fast is not to sleep through those times, or to fill them with more work; but rather to utilize that time for prayer, conversation, meditation, and focused consideration. It's advisable that you premeditate what your focus during this period will be. It may be a pressing issue in your life, a major decision you're seeking direction for, a lifestyle change you desire to make, or maybe, and always a great idea, just a desire to get closer to God. But fasting and the exercising of disciplines is most effective when one prepares, prays and creates time to listen.

FASTING TYPES

There are three primary types of biblical based fasting: Full fast, Partial fast, and the Daniel fast. A full fast is reflected by no eating of any food and only the consumption of liquids during the designated period of abstaining. During a full fast, it's important to know the state of your health and to make sure you respond appropriately in the event of a physical decline. A partial fast is generally executed from sun-up to sundown or from the time you awake until a designated time in the evening. This fast generally includes abstaining from some foods but not all, and maintaining the consumption of fluids. For example, the exemption of fried foods, sweets, and red meats could be considered a partial fast. Remember, choosing foods and drinks that you actually enjoy are the best way to engage in a partial fast. Lastly, there's the Daniel fast, which is a form of a partial fast. The Daniel Fast involves abstaining from all meats and sweets while consuming water, juice, fruits, grains, and vegetables. This fast is very detailed, so please consult either someone with experience or research the specifications prior to engaging. Fasting and Disciplines will sometimes go hand in hand as you start these different experiences. Remember to plan it out and see it through.

Additionally, biblical based fasting is generally seen in four different time spans; 3 days, 7 days, 21 days, and 40 days. While these are the typical standards, don't be afraid to make adjustments as necessary. Remember the most important part of your Christian relationship is sincerity. It's important that you keep this in perspective so that you set realistic goals for yourself as you began your fasting journey. Your partial fast may start with extracting one meal a day, or your full fast maybe for two days. The most important thing is keeping your heart and mind connected to your moment and realizing that God is more concerned with the authenticity of your heart and sincerity of your sacrifice.

WILL GOD SPEAK?

As one begins engages in this moment of sacrifice, don't fall into the trap of focusing so much on God-inspired solutions that you invest little into the sacrifice. Often the biggest misconception is that fasting is used singularly to "hear from God." However, I suggest that not only is this a seeking moment to hear from God but an opportunity for us to process our own thoughts effectively and make well thought out decisions that are God-inspired by way of wisdom and authenticity. The Bible says in Proverbs 11:14 *"Without wise leadership, a nation falls; there is safety in having many advisers."* And Proverbs 12:15 states, *"Fools think their own way is right, but the wise listen to others."* Both of these scriptures encourage us to hear from others and to utilize not solely the voice of God as a resource for good decision making, but also the resource of wise people around us as a means of guidance. A season of fasting or discipline is a great opportunity to connect with those individuals in your life and get their counsel on the various issues you may be fasting for or operating in a discipline for. Accordingly, I've used the phrase

60

"pure thoughts" a few times up until this point in this chapter. I do so to suggest that sometimes during a moment of such sacrifice the objective is also to create space and opportunity for us to think clearly on a particular area of our lives that well, you guessed it, lacks clarity. Abstaining from the various influences we encounter in some of our most comfortable environments is sometimes necessary for us to filter our decisions through our personal convictions and values. Let's be honest. We live in a fast-paced world that keeps us running around, unfocused, and constantly sends us messages that are designed to influence our decision making. What fasting and disciplines also give you the opportunity to do is "think for yourself"! That sacrifice of time in one area is now substituted with moments of "pure thinking"; thought that is filtered through wise counsel, authentic understanding of self, and honest self-evaluation. Sometimes you're waiting on God to speak, while he's waiting for you to discover!

HEALTHY DECISIONS

As God constantly pushes us towards wisdom, it must not go without address that you must make healthy decisions when deciding to fast. Evaluate your medical history and consult physicians when necessary to determine what fast will be right for you. God doesn't want you to sacrifice meals at the expense of your well being, rather he wants you to find ways to honor your commitment to the relationship that will make you available not just spiritually, but mentally, physically, and emotionally as well.

STAYING MOTIVATED

If you're like me, we've been down this road before! Excited about fasting, start the process, start to see everything you want and can't have, start making compromises, and before long, you've checked out early! During my spiritual journey fasting has probably been the hardest area for me to grab hold of and remain consistent. With that in mind, I've come up with a couple things that have helped me stay motivated and focused while participating in fast or disciplines. Find some accountability partners! Historically, fasting is a process intended to be private and confidential until completion. This is an element I still suggest employing, which means no status', mass text, snap chat struggles, or every time someone offers you something you don't have to publicize you're fasting. However, I know when I first began I struggled because I had no one to call on to encourage me to keep going or to join with me. Finding someone to fast with you is the easiest way to get going. It's just like having a gym partner, you want to go, but it makes it easier when someone is on the treadmill next to you. I sincerely believe God wants you just to get it going and has designed the Christian journey for corporate worship through various forms. It gives you a resource not only for encouragement but for prayer and conversation as well. In the event that someone you trust can't actively do the fast with you, still having them as a source of encouragement may provide that extra push when you feel like giving up.

Remind yourself daily of your purpose! In the midst of trying to let go of things that are apart of your normal routine, frustration and doubt can easily set in. The most dangerous moment in any fast is forgetting why you're fasting in the first place. It's that guidance, closeness, or intervention you're seeking that drives this sacrifice! Once you lose the goal, it becomes difficult to stay motivated. You can maintain this in a few practical ways. Set a reminder on your phone, computer, or somewhere else that consistently has your attention to keep you focused on the purpose of your fast. You can also have set prayer times with an accountability partner. This moment of accountability will serve as a constant reinforcement of why you've entered into this moment of sacrifice. Lastly, journal your experience. It has been noted that writing things physically significantly implants them in our minds as it involves a process of thought not required by just speaking. Utilizing these principles can help to connect you to the process daily and refuel you for the days ahead.

All in all, enjoy the journey into a deeper relationship with God. Fasting enables you to clear out space and time for intimate moments that otherwise get overlooked by the hustle and bustle of everyday life. It is in these moments we see how far our love goes and that we're able to grow in both wisdom and maturity. Remember, fasting and disciplines are no competition; set a goal, stick to it, and enjoy the ride. You'll have a sense of accomplishment upon completion that no words can describe.

The Fasting Devotional

Ezra 8:23
23 So we fasted and earnestly prayed that our God would take care of us, and he heard our prayer.

In a distracted world, it's rare to find focus these days. Between CNN updates, text messages, social media accounts, phone calls on both our work phone and our personal phone, and let's not even talk about Netflix. I mean they go into the next episode so quickly that you almost feel guilty not to watch an entire season in two days. If we're not careful, we can suffer from Death by Distraction. And what often suffers most is our spiritual health and progression. Fasting centers us and puts us in a posture of intimacy with God. It challenges us to eliminate the desires of the body so we can give attention to the desires of the heart. We neglect food for the body so we can feed the spirit. We exercise disciplines so we can control our lives instead of our lives controlling us. Some fast is necessary for revelation, others just for reconciliation, and yet other just for lighting a fire in our relationship with God. No matter your "why," there's nothing like a temporary sacrifice to sustain a long-term commitment. Fasting works...give it a try.

Reflection Questions:

What are some areas of your life where you feel like fasting could be the appropriate response?

Who are people in your life that could support you fasting or exercising a discipline?

How will you plan to incorporate fasting or disciplines into your life in the year to come?

Inside-Out:

_____
_____
_____
_____
_____
_____
_____
_____
_____
_____
_____
_____
_____
_____

Devotional Prayer

The Prayer of Jabez (1 Chronicles 4:10)
"Oh, that you would bless me and expand my territory! Please be with me in all that I do, and keep me from all trouble and pain!" And God granted him his request. Today I expect your blessings, and I expect God-like expansion. God be with me in all that I do and protect my heart, mind, and soul.
In Jesus Name, Amen.

THE CHURCH CHAPTER
FINDING A PLACE TO CALL HOME

Driving home one evening Ashley and I were hungry, so we decided to stop for something quick to eat. Arriving at a stop light,, we saw several fast food restaurants located on the same corner. Ashley, an avid fan of Chick-Fil-A, wanted chicken. While I was craving my "go-to" meal, Pizza! What struck me as interesting is it wasn't hard for us to determine where to go because we understood what we had an appetite for and which places could satisfy that hunger. I know what you're saying again, "What in the world does this have to do with me finding a church home?" Stay with me just a little bit longer.

As I reflected on the infancy of my ministry, I recall a meeting I had with Bishop K.W. Brown, executive pastor of Mount Lebanon Missionary Baptist Church in Chesapeake, Va. During this meeting Bishop Brown asked me a question that I'll never forget, "Vernon, Why is it that so many fast food restaurants can exist on the same corner no matter where you go?" After a brief pause, I was without an educated response. He gave me his answer, "Because they all understand their co-mission is to provide you with food expeditiously, but their individual missions are unique. One says *"HAVE IT YOUR WAY,"* another says *"EAT FRESH, EVEN LATE,"* while others offer chicken and some don't." He elaborated by saying churches work in a similar fashion. We all are called to offer something different to the people we serve. This concept should also guide us as we seek to plant ourselves in a ministry. The primary focus shouldn't be what we offer, but rather what do you have an appetite for in this season of your life? The more you grow to understand yourself and your needs, the easier it will be to make a good decision about a place to call home. You may be hungry for international missions work, inner-city outreach, Christian education, social justice, or maybe you have a small child, and you're looking for a safe space where they can develop and grow along with others their age. Finding a place that can satisfy your unique hunger is going to produce the healthiest and happiest you. In this chapter, we'll explore the need for church and its people, identify some of the challenges of church transition, and discuss effective ways to grow as an individual in your church journey.

WHAT IS CHURCH?

During the early days of Christianity, it was dangerous to be a follower of Christ. During the time the Bible was written Christianity represented less than 1% of the entire population. Talk about standing out or being the minority! Fellow believers met at houses or designed locations where they sought to grow together in their understanding of God, but also to grow in their relationships with each other. The Greek word for church, Ecclesia literally means "The called out ones." This term did not reference building structures or worship services but rather the individuals that carried the Christian message or brand. In other words, effective "church" searching is less about the name of the building or denomination, but rather how it helps you develop holistically and interpersonally. In this way, the true goal is to find a congregation of believers that help you become a better church! When you embrace the reality that you are the church, you start to see the necessity for knowing your spiritual appetite for this season of your life. As you grow, your appetite may change! Dually, one who understands themselves as the church must not undervalue the need for Christian fellowship. An island needs no help until a flood comes! Don't confuse being the church, with being the lone ranger. I believe God has created us all with great purpose and assignment, but it is through our connection with others that we remain most effective and most energized to bring forth harvest in our lives. What I argue is that it is in understanding your need for interpersonal, spiritual relationships that you truly develop and grow into the church God has called you to be. The best missions are completed with a team!

SEASON OF TRANSITION

Looking at this area of our Christian development is often tricky as we must come to terms with the reality that just like nature has seasons so do our lives.

We must often be reminded that our first commitment is to ensure that all that God placed in us is harvested effectively. This does not mean that we will never encounter conflict or disappointment and that when we do, we should "transition" out of a ministry. But we must be able to evaluate both our personal assignment and personal growth in every season of our life. In every season you should produce a new harvest, when you cannot see the fruits of that season, you must evaluate yourself, your environments, and your relationships. When it comes to our churches, many of us take on one of three expressions: the loyalists, the commentator, and the nomad.

Let's start with the Loyalists, typically characterized by one who has a longstanding personal connection with a particular church, or they have very strong ties to persons who belong to a church. This individual generally finds it difficult to transition due to their feeling of obligation and responsibility to the ministry, even if the church no longer effectively helps them grow in their spiritual development. Often this person feels as if their transition will bring offense to someone else. So to avoid conflict and delay discomfort, they stay put hoping that what they feel would change. It's important to note, we all need loyalist in our midst, but it's also important that we honor the voice of change in our life and the Holy Spirit's prompting when appropriate.

The Commentator comes next, characterized by one who lacks church commitments because they are always looking for the "perfect church." By nature, this individual is typically analytical and tends to see fault in most everything. Commentators are great at that you know. They're paid to pay attention to the details. The first moment one of these persons encounters a bad Sunday, challenging member, or a moment of offense, they decide that this isn't the place for them. As important as knowing what you do need is knowing what you can live without. Is music ministry vital to you? Are you in search for small groups to grow in? Do you feel like you need a woman's ministry? Are you looking for a place where other young adults worship regularly? Continue to find clarity in your needs and don't allow things that aren't a priority for you to limit your growth. Likened to children who don't eat their vegetables (I was that type of kid); the rest of the plate has things you want and need, but if it touches the green stuff you'll throw it all away. Be careful that you're not throwing away fulfilling ministries because you only see the "green stuff" in them.

Finally comes the Nomad, typically characterized by one who lacks the ability to commit to a ministry for one of two reasons. The first stems from a misunderstanding of what church is supposed to provide, thus attaching to a ministry seems pointless to this individual. Additionally, this lack of ministry commitment also may come from church scars that have never been healed by way of direct or indirect exposure. In summary, someone who just doesn't feel they can trust the church or can't readily identify the value of Church. This individual's greatest challenge is to remind themselves that they are the church, and to be fruitful you must connect with other believers. The strength of a garden is not in one plant's roots alone, but when those can stretch and connect with others. In a healthy garden, it's difficult to pull out one plant, because of how the roots are connected in growing ground. Never underestimate the value of who you are connected to, this is the power of the Church.

VISION AND MISSION

Determining a church home can still be a difficult process, especially when we don't ask the right questions. It's important that as you discern you look beyond superficial factors. While evaluating the choir, the sermons, how they take up offering, what you have to wear to go there, and if you feel engaged and comfortable, rarely do I find people ask about the "Vision and Mission" of the church. Don't get me wrong; I think all of the things as mentioned earlier are important too. But let's take a moment and examine the value of the vision and mission for a moment. Vision in its simplest form is what we plan to do as a congregation or organization. It is the ultimate objective that the leadership has set forth for a particular assembly. This aspect of the congregation is typically long term but can help you identify if your interest can be sustained as apart of that particular ministry. Have you ever got in your car to travel somewhere and you pull out your GPS, only to realize you don't have the address for where you're going? Without this critical piece of information, guided direction is impossible. Vision works similarly in that it is the final destination for a ministry or the place they want to get to. If unidentified or unclear, it may be difficult for you to determine if you want to take the ride. However, when you believe in the destination, it becomes easier to believe in the direction that comes with it.

When you're disconnected from the vision of a ministry, you'll find struggle in taking direction. Additionally, the mission of a ministry is how they intend to get there or the things they do to bring their vision to past. This may come in the form of programs, events, community initiatives, giving plans, and many other forms of progress. Generally speaking, one's mission is to complete specific goals to move them closer to completion of the ultimate objective. When seeking out a ministry to join you must ask yourself do these goals connect with who I am as an individual. I encourage anyone that is considering joining a ministry, don't be afraid to ask questions. It is only when you see clearly that you can drive full speed ahead! If you clearly identify with a local assembly, you'll find your ability to become active and effective much easier, much sooner.

MEGA (church) or MINI (church):

Within our conversation about church this chapter we've hopefully developed a greater understanding of what "church" truly is all about. However, this question is extremely popular and mustn't go unaddressed, megachurch or smaller church? I think the answer lies in our original analogy at the beginning of this chapter. I wouldn't go to Burger King and ask for a Big Mac because I recognize they do not specialize in producing that sandwich. The focus should not be on size but effectiveness! Am I able to see the mission and vision effectively carried out? Does this ministry challenge me and motivate me to grow as a person? Is this where God is leading me to be? Two temptations always create challenges when this question comes about - popularity and patience. Typically, the popularity of larger churches draws a lot of membership, but very few people are involved in "making it all happen." I've often heard people say I want to go somewhere where people will know me, and that's great. But one of the important things to remember is you'll get out of every experience what you put into it! Don't expect to be known if you sit in the back, rarely speak, leave early, and never get involved. This is true for any size ministry. You must put forth the effort to grow! I believe most churches, of all sizes, have someone who wants to connect and collaborate, but our ability to avail ourselves has a direct impact on the effectiveness. All I'm suggesting is be sure to stretch yourself beyond your comfort zone.

Furthermore, it is tempting to leave a smaller church because of the resources another ministry might have to do what you want to do now and not later. Remember that you shouldn't connect to a ministry for what you're bringing to it but rather what it's bringing to you. You're not joining a church to grow them you're joining a place that can grow you. By consequence, you then bring your gifts and abilities to said community to support the vision and mission being fulfilled. Be reminded that if you connect with the goals and objectives of a ministry and feel as if you're growing, be patient in allowing God to work that vision through you. God might have given it to you but that doesn't mean right now is the time to harvest. It will be much more fulfilling if you plant the idea in the soil that God has pre-destined for it to grow in. Ultimately, finding a church home is more about finding "you" than it is "it"! By identifying yourself as the church, you must believe that God has called you to great things. He has purposed you to carry his spirit, his message, and his love throughout the world. Finding a place to grow and develop into the church God has called you to be is essential to your journey. We all need watering, harvesting, encouragement, and sometimes even to be challenged to produce the best fruit possible. Get planted in a good place and GROW!

The Church Devotional

Hebrews 10:24-25
24 Let us think of ways to motivate one another to acts of love and good works. 25 And let us not neglect our meeting together, as some people do, but encourage one another, especially now that the day of his return is drawing near.

One of my favorite movies growing up was "The Wizard Of Oz." One concept that drove the movie was Dorothy's pursuit of "home." As she nears the end of her journey, she finds out that the very thing she sought from Oz she had the power to produce all along, the ability to go home by the clicking of her heels and declaration of "There's no place like home." She wanted to consume but had the power to create. Today I challenge you to remember that Church is more than a place we go, it's what we are. That we've all been called together not to just "have church" but to leave and "be church." And just like Dorothy, we may be seeking to consume what we are called to create. I encourage you today, don't neglect meeting together, but let the gathering motivate us to change the world.

Reflection Questions:

What does it mean to you to "Be The Church"?

What is your appetite or need in this season of your life?

In what ways will you "be the church" for someone this week?

Inside-Out:

_____
_____
_____
_____
_____
_____
_____
_____
_____
_____
_____
_____
_____

Devotional Prayer

THE LORD'S PRAYER (Matthew 6:9-13)
Our Father in heaven,
Hallowed be Your name.
Your kingdom come.
Your will be done
On earth, as it is in heaven.
Give us this day our daily bread.
And forgive us our debts,
As we forgive our debtors.
And do not lead us into temptation,
But deliver us from the evil one.
For Yours is the kingdom and the power
and the glory forever. Amen.

THE TEMPTATION CHAPTER
DEALING WITH DESIRES AND DISCIPLINES

In earlier chapter's I've mentioned that I have two small children, Madison and Jackson, whom I love dearly. But parenting, well I believe the language I chose earlier was "joyful inconvenience." I mean don't get me wrong, it's wonderful and all, but I really miss talking in complete sentences. You heard me right! Having a two-year-old and three year old in the house means your sentences are assassinated by time-sensitive instruction daily. And if they are complete sentences, they are phrases you often say that you don't even consider them quality adult statements any longer. It sounds something like this, *"Don't you dare," "No, not that," "Come here," "Now," "Wait wait wait wait," "Stop," "Stop Again," "How many times do I have to tell you?" "What did you say?",* well, you get the point. A huge part of guiding my children to a healthy life is making sure they don't harm themselves because they couldn't see the dangers I could. Ironically, I believe the same thing lies at the core of biblical disciplines and boundaries. God sees the danger, and protects us but placing boundaries in our life. It's in the tension between our desires and these boundaries that temptation arises.

It's important to note; temptation is no respecter of persons. It does not take into consideration our age, gender, ethnicity, or economic status before it attacks. Temptation pursues us, pressures us, and persuades us to fracture our relationship with God and his will. The truth is temptation is after one thing, your life. The life awaiting you that is greater than anything you've ever imagined, and the enemy is counting on enough distractions, disappointments, or downfalls to deter you from pursuing it. Jesus says it like this in *John 10:10: A thief is only there to steal and kill and destroy. I came so they can have real and eternal life, more and better life than they ever dreamed of.* The best of life that God has for us brings more than momentary satisfaction but a lifetime of fulfillment. And this is why we call Satan the "tempter," because his existence is dedicated to pulling us away from the Life Jesus has sacrificed to give us access to. A life that is worth every sacrifice and struggle that we may feel to achieve righteousness. In this chapter, we'll explore the strategies of temptation, the need for boundaries, and the hard truth about temptation.

THE HARD TRUTH

Temptation is defined as the desire to do something wrong or unwise. We love to focus on the former word but not the latter. Because that would mean temptation is not solely about sin, but sometimes it's about wisdom. Temptation launches attacks on both the purity of our lives and the quality of our life. When we only focus on the attacks against our purity and not our quality of life we leave ourselves vulnerable in our spiritual fulfillment. To when the battle of sexual purity but not the battle of financial stewardship is still a tragedy, to win the battle of drug addiction but not the battle of food addiction is still a tragedy, to win the battle of profanity but not the battle of positive affirmation over insecurity is still a tragedy. Every temptation is not designed to prevent you from seeing heaven. Some temptations are designed to keep you from seeing heaven on earth. All too often we highlight how to maintain spiritual purity, but God also wants us to walk in wisdom and spiritual authority; authority that cannot be sustained if we don't win the battle of both purity and quality Additionally, and here's the hard truth, temptation will never leave. You can't praise your way through it, pray your way away from it, faith your way over it, and whatever else cliche that you'd like to apply. Here's where I believe our theology has somewhat ill-prepared us for this battle. Temptation is consistent. It just evolves based on our spiritual and human maturity. As we overcome, resist, and manage it better at one level, it reintroduces itself at another. The single struggles with sex before marriage, and assumes temptation will disappear once becoming a spouse. Only to find that while sex may no longer be the temptation, now stewardship is. Or we overcome the temptation of laziness, but now promoted to deal with the temptation of integrity. Or maybe you struggle with the temptation of gossip, only to overcome it and deal with the temptation of pride. God's design for life is inclusive of temptation, and while he does not tempt us, he does allow it. I'll prove it to you in scripture.

In Genesis, Satan the tempter comes as a snake to tempt Eve to eat from the tree in the middle of the Garden of Eden. Pause right there, if God didn't want them eating from tree why allow it to remain in the Garden. And of all places, in the middle of the garden. Could it be that God will allow you to see the temptation but not touch it because every time you look but don't touch you affirm your commitment to God and not to self? Even Jesus once baptized was taken by the Spirit of God into the wilderness where Satan tempted him for 40 days. Notice when you read that passage of scripture that the "S" in spirit was capitalized signifying a reflection of the holy spirit. Ok let's pause again, so the Holy Spirit our comforter leads Jesus to be tempted. But that doesn't seem very comfortable, does it? Because could it be that commitment must always confirm calling. And commitment can only be confirmed by our ability to manage temptation on every level. Temptation may not leave, but you can elevate above the present level.

BLESSINGS AND BOUNDARIES

I had a dog named Shadow when I was a kid. I loved Shadow. He was playful, obedient, and loyal. One day we came home from church to find several of my neighbors and childhood friends assembled around our gate. Upon approach, saw Shadow, lying motionless on the ground with various table foods around him. Apparently, they had been feeding Shadow an array of foods from their homes, and when we received the autopsy report, the told us Shadow died because he was continuously fed food that he was not designed to digest. I'd like you to consider this, what if you're killing your life, trying to digest things you're not designed for. What if some habits, people, and environments are killing your life. And God is trying to protect you by placing boundaries around your life based on your design.

What is a design? It is the look or highest function of a thing. So if we are God's creation, his design, his handiwork, wouldn't he know how we should function best? When the fish is out of the water for too long, it dies. If the plant rooted deeply in soil gets plucked, eventually it dies. If a butterfly falls from its chrysalis, and cannot be hung again, eventually it dies. Notice that in these instances, the fish doesn't see the water as a boundary, but a blessing. It recognizes that it was designed to breathe best in the water and other environments may offer temporary exploration but eventual expiration if not returned to the environment most necessary for its survival. The plant doesn't see the soil as a boundary but as a blessing. Even though it is immobile, it recognizes that through the soil the roots absorb rain, and being in the right soil means the right growth. It may be stationary, but it's not stagnant. And the caterpillar does not see it's chrysalis (cocoon) as a boundary, but as a blessing, because if it honors this temporary conferment, the outcome is transformation into the butterfly. What am I suggesting? Design matters and all things created by God were created with boundaries.

The truth is Christian disciplines are not always easy. They ask us to deny was is desirable to our bodies and minds often. But how we see these moments of self-imposed discipline or delay make all the difference in the world. You could see it as no or not now. When God delays desire, it produces the best in us maybe not in the moment but definitely for our future. If you look with the right perspective, you just may find that the boundary is really a blessing.

THE STRATEGIES OF TEMPTATION

So how you do you plan to overcome temptation, by proactively guarding against its strategies. Here's some good news for you, temptation is pretty consistent. If we look at the words penned in 1 John 2:16-17 it says:
16 For everything in the world—the lust of the flesh, the lust of the eyes, and the pride of life—comes not from the Father but from the world. 17 The world and its desires pass away, but whoever does the will of God lives forever. There are three distinct strategies of temptation that we must also be aware of. The first is the lust of the flesh or the craving for physical pleasure. Let me be the first to admit, I was not a virgin when I got married, I struggled with pornography controlling my life, and I was promiscuous in my collegiate life. The craving for physical pleasure controlled me, but never fulfilled me. I couldn't understand why my body constantly screamed for more, but my heart screamed out for less. Because I was not designed for that behavior, and once I found joy in the boundary I found life. Did that mean I didn't struggle, have desires, or have to constantly pray against temptation? Not at all, I had to do that daily, but I learned to find self-control in my life, and realized God wasn't saying never, he was just saying not right now.

Additionally, temptation is introduced by the lust of the eyes. In a culture that scrolls, studies the lives of others, and seeks sameness, we find that the lust of the eyes has caused many to fall. This is most often where the spirit of compromise dwells, prompting us to become or duplicate what we see most. To altar identity and authenticity, to sacrifice sincerity for sameness, because sight often drives compromise more than any other temptation. This overexposure of sight drives lust into our minds and hearts, and if not disciplined can plant seeds of destruction deeply. But as we manage our eyes and our spirits we must constantly apply a filter to our lives to help process our daily intake. It also can't be unstated that we must invite the Holy Spirit into our lives to convict and discard that which will not feed our spiritual growth.

Finally, temptation sneaks up on us through the pride of life. This strategy can manipulate us in one of two ways. The first and most common is the pursuit of popularity, prominence, and prosperity outside of God's will. Notice I didn't say prominence or prosperity were bad themselves, but when we pursue desires outside of God's will or design, that's when we're at the greatest danger to drown in desire. The pride of life prompts us to pursue the success as mentioned above for all the wrong reasons. Because titles come, money comes, status comes, and all the while peace remains missing, joy is absent, and fulfillment is fleeing. But culture will tell us to get more while God is saying come get me. The pride of life also doesn't allow for us to invite support into our lives. So often, we mask our true emotions and experiences, for fear that no one can handle our reality. And so we settle for presenting the fantasy while we suffer in silence. The beauty of Jesus is grace has already covered our secrets, struggles, and stains, so never allow pride to keep you from pursuing the love of Christ. Pride will keep you bound, but Christ will set you free.

Ultimately, temptation is unavoidable, but that doesn't mean it's insurmountable. The greater our awareness of the strategies of sin and temptation, the stronger we become. And as we learn to see blessings in our boundaries, we'll find greater joy in what it means to honor God with our lives. Today is a great day to conquer temptation, and to say boldly, my body, my eyes, and my pride won't control me, I will control it. You've got this, and we're praying for you.

The Temptation Devotional

Hebrews 12:1
11 No discipline is enjoyable while it is happening—it's painful! But afterward, there will be a peaceful harvest of right living for those who are trained in this way.

I LOVE WORKING OUT. But I hate eating well. And that my friends is the only thing standing in my way of my 8pack of abs. I'm sure many of you can relate to setting goals and trying to make the subtle adjustments that will turn that vision a reality. It may not be physically, but it could be emotionally, socially, financially or spiritually. But that desire to go from concept to reality is consistent in all of our lives. The truth is overcoming temptation is about a daily dose of discipline. It's about keeping the goal front and center and making temporary sacrifices for a lifetime of fulfillment. God's not now is not a never, and his delay is not denial. Stay strong and believe that the harvest will come.

Reflection Questions:

What is your great temptation in this season of your life?

What are some boundaries you can put in place to overcome these obstacles?

Who are two people in your life you can both ask and trust to help you navigate your inner struggles?

Inside-Out:

_____

_____

_____

_____

_____

_____

_____

_____

_____

_____

_____

_____

_____

Devotional Prayer;

Lord help me overcome the temptation of _____
_____. *Holy Spirit, I invite you into my life
to help me fight my temptations. I want to pursue righteousness and holiness in areas
of weakness. I cannot do this in my humanity, but with your power, I can overcome
every temptation. I commit to disciplining my life for your will, and joyfully embrace
boundaries as a blessing. Protect me from myself, my desires, and my flesh. I resist the
urge to chase temporary satisfaction but instead pray for the strength to seek life-long
fulfillment. I pursue purity today in my body, my thoughts, and my heart. This will
be the best season of my life because I will walk in self-control. Desire will no longer
control me. I will control its place in my life. With the help of the Holy Spirit, I am
FREE. In Jesus Name, Amen.*

THE FAITH CHAPTER
BUILDING FAITH ONE STEP AT A TIME

The At the age of 10 years old I was like any other kid you would meet. I loved playing with my friends, sports, video games, and asking a lot of questions. But my life would change would dramatically this year as I took a trip to a local park with my family. It was on this day that I would suffer a fracture, and upon further review, it would be determined that I had Osteogenic Sarcoma, a rare form of bone cancer that was extremely aggressive. I didn't know it then, but my faith would be stretched in unimaginable ways over the next decade as I learned how to navigate a life of uncertainty, disability, and spiritual mistrust. That's right, my immediate reaction to being diagnosed with cancer, constant threats of losing my leg, and a pessimistic prognosis, at ten years old was not "faith-filled." I was afraid, and if I'm completely honest, mad at God. I felt like everything I had been told in church up until the point was a lie. Where was the protector, the promise keeper, the provider, the healer, the champion that I saw people shout about every Sunday? I wish I could tell you I snapped out of it quickly, but the truth is it only got worse. I saw the pain in my parents' eyes and the fear of my family. And I continued to question deeper how God could claim love for us and allow this to be our reality. After all the prayers I heard and prophecies I received in the hospital room, to see no change in my physical condition was demoralizing. This was the beginning of my Christianity.

Growing up in church you hear a lot of language around the topic of faith. Whether through church cliches like *"He may not come when you want him, but he'll be there right on time."* Or through testimony service that could be 3 minutes or 3 hours. Faith is affirmed as a pillar of our Christian walk. And rightfully so, in Hebrews 11:6 it says: *"And it is impossible to please God without faith"*. I think the passage is pretty self-explanatory. However, proclamation and application are not the same things. Declaring faith is not the same as demonstrating faith. It was this reality that I found myself in, and I believe you may find yourself in one day. Trying to exercise your faith in the midst of a season that says be everything but faith-filled. My testimony is not that I just overcame cancer, it's that I figured out early on how to walk through the experience with faith. A faith that didn't just bring me the peace when I arrived at the promise, but I also had peace in the process. Throughout this chapter, I'd like to share four practical ways to develop faith in your own life.

POSITIVE AFFIRMATION

Researchers at Georgia University and the University of Harvard came together to do a study on the power of words. They determined that whenever a word is released from the mouth, it seemed to coincide with a chemical process of the brain forming emotional response. In other words, my mouth and my mind are intimately connected. I want you to know this today that developing faith doesn't start with what you feel. It starts with what you form. This means what you say about your life forms your life. So, if I say I'm broke, broke comes looking for me. If I say, I'm never going to accomplish something motivation is lost and consequently so goes opportunity. However, when I begin to declare I'm enough, I can do this, I am wise, I am qualified, I am confident, I start to live out my affirmations. When I was going through surgery and cancer, I recall my Grandmother repeatedly speaking as if my complete healing was all but a foregone conclusion. I couldn't understand her logic at the time because the medical reports did not align with her affirmation. But after a while, I learned to make affirmations based on the report of the Lord and not the report of man. I can tell you this with confidence; it immediately increased my joy, my confidence, and my hope. Even when my physical condition was the same my mind and mouth were full of faith. Learn how to manage your mouth, and you'll transform your mind, and eventually, your life.

GUARD YOUR CONVERSATIONS

In partnership with personal affirmations, comes protecting your conversations. Friends, family, and associates all play a critical role in faith seasons. They either are contributors to our faith or contradictions. It is difficult to grow your faith when nothing's feeding it. And while you have a personal responsibility to affirm your faith you can't counter all of your productivity by exposing it to negativity. Especially in vulnerable seasons, the guarding of conversations is essential to faith development. Pessimistic people, doubters, and those who are ignorant of the promises of God can't water seeds they've never seen. What does this mean? That some seasons will require the complete subtraction or healthy separation of people from your life. I'm not suggesting that every person who fails to contribute to your faith should no longer be considered "friendship material," but you must be able to discern seasons and the necessity for managing your exposure in these seasons. Your conversations must reinforce the life you're trying to live and the faith you're trying to develop. Guard your conversations, and you'll find that seeds of faith will grow quickly when watered with the right support.

CELEBRATE SMALL WINS

It would probably be appropriate at this point to define faith for our corporate understanding. Here's my definition: *a choice to live in commitment to one's truth in spite of conflict.* I ascribe to this definition for two reasons. First, because the affirmation of God and our belief in his will and authority requires faith in and of itself. We stand as Christians to proclaim that we trust God is at work even when we don't understand what he's doing. It's this truth that undergirds our choices and provides confidence and comfort in the face of uncertain experiences. But equally as important as faith in God, is faith in self. So while faith may lead me to spiritual truth and commitment to God, I have to see the same truth in my self to live out God's purpose for my life.

We see this internal faith conflict played out in Numbers 13 as the spies go to observe the promise land. When they returned to report, they discouraged progression even after God's promise because of how they saw themselves. In verse 33 the spies state, *"We saw the Nephilim there. We seemed like grasshoppers in our own eyes, and we looked the same to them."* I always wondered how they could know what they looked like to them without conversation? The answer is right above, and it always is, how do you see yourself with your own eyes? External conflict is inevitable, culturally, socially, economically, and physically. But there is no threat to your faith development like internal

82

conflict. Faith says I see me the way God sees me.

In fairness, this is a daily challenge for us all. Which is why I affirm in this section to celebrate the small wins. You may not go from total insecurity to total belief, but if you can start to celebrate small faith accomplishments, it will build your fortitude. If you've always wanted to write a book, stop halfway and celebrate the progress. Have you always felt God called you to record an album, don't celebrate fourteen tracks, release an EP and celebrate the release of three songs? Maybe you're going through a difficult season financially or physically, celebrate a good report, or a bill paid off. Celebrate a milestone in physical therapy or a month you didn't go over budget. Faith is built not bought. And as you start to see your faith grow, you can celebrate along the way your progress even before the promise.

ACT IT OUT

Finally, faith isn't faith until you put it into action. Did you know the word faith in the greek is both a noun and verb (Pistis and Pistevo)? Meaning faith is more than an adjective. It's defined by activity. We see this narrative throughout the biblical literature. Peter exercises faith when he steps out of the boat to walk on water. David exercises faith when he steps beyond the front lines to fight Goliath. Gideon exercises faith when he decides to accept a leadership position that he's extremely under qualified for. Moses exercises faith when he goes back to his hometown to be an activist when he could've remained comfortable neglecting the needs of his people. Faith is about action. Building our faith is about the courage to act out the thing that God has placed on our heart. Maybe it's activism. Maybe it's artistry, maybe it's just smiling while you're surviving, or walking with pride when your financial landscape should have your ashamed. Faith prompts us to act following our promise and not our present. This is not always easy, but the more you walk in faith, honoring your truth, and trusting the process, the more powerful your life becomes. Ultimately, I hope you would commit to growing your faith today. I can't close this chapter out without letting you know that kid with cancer, who they thought would die is writing this book today. Thirteen surgeries, three years of chemotherapy, and several brushes with death later I'm living my best life. Healthier than I've ever been, stronger both internally and externally than I've ever been, and more committed than ever before to choose my truth every single day of my life. I don't know what next step awaits you, but I'm confident God is waiting for you outside of the boat. You will find that the more steps you take, the more confidence you'll get. And even though Peter sank at the end, he could celebrate that he took more steps on the water than any other disciple. The water is waiting, step out on faith.

The Faith Devotional

Hebrews 11:1-2
1 Faith shows the reality of what we hope for; it is the evidence of things we cannot see.
2 Through their faith, the people in days of old earned a good reputation.

I love the game *"Heads Up."* If you've never played it, there's plenty of family fun to go around. My favorite category is *"Act it Out."* If you've never seen your Grandparent acting out animals and questionable activities you're missing out on life. The point is, everyone is investing their all to display something they can't use their words to convey. I believe faith is one of those areas that require more than our words but our actions. The world doesn't believe we have faith because we say it, they believe it when we "Act It Out." I want to encourage you today to stay committed to your truth. The water is waiting for you to step out of the boat. And even if you sink, just take the step. God will catch you every time.

Reflection Questions:

Do you struggle with living committed to your truth? If so, why?

Who are people you can talk to fuel your faith?

What is one way you can act out your faith this coming week?

Inside-Out:

_____
_____
_____
_____
_____
_____
_____
_____
_____
_____
_____
_____

Devotional Prayer

I am created by God. My life, my gifts, my hopes, and dreams are valuable in this world. I believe in who I am and who I am becoming and that I haven't seen the best of my life yet. I am FAVORED by God in every area of my life. I am committed to feeding my BELIEF today with the Word of God, the power of Wisdom, and the Will of an Overcomer. God has not given me a spirit of fear, but of love, power, and a sound mind. So I cast out all doubt, and respond to the presence of fear with the power of faith. I honor my truth and identity today and refuse to accept a life less than my intended design and destiny. I may not see it yet, but I can feel it! I may not deserve it, but by grace I declare it. I may not have all the resources I need, but I have the provider. I may not have a good report, but I have the healer. I may not have the network, but I have the door opener. I may not have the education, but I have the source of all wisdom. God created me, loves me, has chosen me, and advocates on my behalf. As long as I have God, I have more than enough. Today I walk in Faith! In Jesus Name, Amen.

THE FORMATION CHAPTER
(RACE, RELIGION, AND RELEVANCE)

Make no mistake about it, from the beginning we've been ONE NATION, DIVIDED, OVER GOD. One God yes, but never have we been one church. How could we? Both our introduction to Christianity and interpretation of the Gospel are rooted in our unique exposures and experiences. To ignore the reality that we have prayed different prayers, sang different songs, and worshipped under different circumstances is to avoid the hard truth of Christianity in America. Consequently, we have been left with a fragmented faith tradition that is now seeking reconciliation with great intensity. This chapter is of great value because if authenticity is to be the bedrock of personal faith than spiritual formation must be apart of every believer's life. Spiritual formation being defined as the practices or processes one takes to progress in their spiritual or religious life. But the practices and processes of discipleship in all our churches are heavily influenced by our ethnicity. With racial reconciliation being a central focus of our time we must continue to create avenues where cultural competency can be explored with openness and inclusiveness. We cannot sacrifice religious identity for the cause of religious integration. In this chapter, we'll explore the relationship of religion and relevance based on ethnic context. While this could be a book in and of itself, we'll explore this topic on a surface level with hopes of understanding how our expression and engagement with the "world" can be impacted by our race.

As we move forward I think it's important to state the obvious; I am an African American man. This means I cannot communicate the position of any other religious experience with the great integrity. So please hear my heart when I say, what is written in this chapter is not a comprehensive view of how all church should be, but prayerfully is a catalyst to Christian communities for conversation and change. Likewise, I can assure you I raise my positions with a heart for diversity and as an advocate of unity. And here's why, because of my grandfather Milburn Turner! Milburn was a white man from Bath Springs, Tennessee who married my black grandmother in the sixties. If that wasn't enough to give people a heart attack, this navy man who served his country but found love outside of the accepted standards of it, not only married this black woman but took her three black children as his own, my mother of which was the eldest. They went on to have two children of their own who were mixed. One of my uncles married a woman from Sierra Leone, West Africa and yet another married a woman from Puerto Rico. Why do I share this with you? To provide context to my heart for this chapter. I've experienced great intimacy and trust with someone from the majority culture. And I've experienced the power of diversity in my own life. But if we are to achieve religious reconciliation there must first be an appreciation for that which makes us different. This chapter is not an attempt to divide, but my attempt to bring about cultural awareness and appreciation for the church as I know it. With hopes that we all might continue to find joy in what makes us different, and the courage to collaborate in building what God is doing for the future.

EXPRESSION

Our first stop on this tour, expression. As a musician, I use to hear the referencing of "Black Church" vs. "White Church" all the time. When most people speak of this contrast, they are referring to superficial factors such as song selection and varied expressions of praise and worship. If you've ever been to a traditional black church, you immediately know some of these variances I'm referring to. It's what W.E.B. Dubois highlighted in *'The Souls of Black Folks'* when noting the three things characterizing the religion of the slave. The preacher, the music, and the frenzy (what he later referred to as "shouting"). These expressions, intensified by years of struggle and adversity coupled with unyielding hope and confidence in God produced an experience on American soil that we know as the black church. Preaching in the minority experience is one of the most highly anticipated parts of any service. Characterized by passion and personality, it is the preacher's job to do more than an exposition of the biblical text, but to also exegete culture and societal struggles of the parishioner. This infusion of hope requires an awareness of the context and perceptions of the minority in America. Because churches have been one of the few places where minorities can collectively be together and unapologetically open about their opinions, the preacher has always carried the weight of being much more than a Sunday morning voice, but one that must carry throughout politics, social justice, community conversations, and the more.

The music of the minority church is passionate and liberating. It is driven by experience and emotion more than anything else. Therefore, it involves frequent repetition and is laced with liberties. This repetitious style has been with us since the beginning of our time in America. Harriet Tubman would sing songs like *'Wade in the Water'* to help escaping slaves know to get in the water to avoid the scent of the dogs. Other songs would be used to tell slaves to come out of hiding, but only if the refrain was sung multiple times was it safe. Nat Turner was known to sing *'Steal Away'* as a sign that a meeting was about to take place to prepare for a revolt. Music has always created the necessary space to feel deeply. For minorities in the American church, this momentary feeling of relief was vital to the church experience. The feeling of released pressure and pain far outweighed the value of elaborate production schedules. Remember, for the minority, the church has historically been the only place of peace, refuge, and respect they had. In other words, there was no rush to get back to life beyond.

And we can't forget about the frenzy, the shouting, the responsiveness, the freedom, all creating an atmosphere of joy, empowerment, and hope. Environments that helped the minority remain connected to a home that was not America, and maintain a measure of identity in a country where every other act is one of assimilation. While in Europe I ministered in song at a Ghanian church. To see their freedom in movement and dancing was life-giving. When the service was over, I told one of the gentlemen, *"This would have never happened in the States."* To which he replied, *"You all claim freedom of your spirit, but have not set free your body."* This is the heart of the minority church's frenzy. Those memories of where we've been will prompt a praise of thanksgiving. And a praise of expectation will drive us where we're going.

ENGAGEMENT

Let me be clear; I do not argue that the aforementioned style of church is better. I also don't argue that it is worse. I argue that it just is what it is, an authentic and honest reflection of the minorities history and daily experience in America. The minority church has always had to be much more than a Sunday gathering. It's had to be a place for food services, academic empowerment, financial literacy, and social services. It's been a center of hope for community and a resource for refuge. Thus, creating an expectation for community and cultural engagement at an intimate level. But it is with much fear that I write this chapter today. Fear that we are losing both influence and connection with those who need it the most.

While there are many areas by which I see this decline, probably most alarming to me is through the social justice movement. With countless tragedies in recent years centered around race and justice, it's vitally important that the church not lose its voice and remain contributors to the narrative. I would dare say this has been the draw, and rightfully so, for many minority Christians away from the church and gospel music. The content and creativity of artist like Kendrick Lamar, J. Cole, and Chance The Rapper, to name a few, have been clear and consistent on the challenges within our culture. But the message of music from Christian sources has remained ambiguous at best on the issues that matter most to minorities in America. We see a growing trait of songs that affirm God's goodness but not our realities. And while I value many of these songs in my worship and affirm their place within the discipleship of all believers, it has been my recent sentiment that I must go outside of the boundaries of Christian genres to find God's voice to a generation about engaging the American experience. Music is not alone in this disconnect, but our sermons have seemingly lost consciousness as well. Relying heavily on the promotion of God's promises but not the responsibilities of God's people. We cannot lose the fire of action and accountability. We are our brother and sister's, keeper. This message must not be lost in the mundanity of religious routine. As you take steps to live more boldly and grow your faith, remember faith is about both our affirmation and our activity. That to engage our world is to be more like Jesus than anything else. It is to remember his presence was seen in the neighborhood far more than in the temple.

Soberly, I ask you to consider your part in being more than a church member, but a movement maker. To see our role as Christians as far greater than our Sunday morning routine but to internalize our responsibility to leave a mark on the world. To see that spiritual formation is to be found in both authenticity and collaboration. While our expressions may differ, and engagement may vary, our hearts must remain united for a time such as this. If we are to change the world, the church must first change within. I encourage us all to hear the heart of the Latino, the Asian, the African, and the Caucasian. Each of us offering our own expressions and engagement, but the kingdom needs us to to be unified more than ever before. The church is still the hope of the world.

The Formation Devotional

Psalms 73:11-12
11 "What does God know?" they ask. "Does the Most High even know what's happening?"

Ephesians 4:3-4
3 Make every effort to keep yourselves united in the Spirit, binding yourselves together with peace. 4 For there is one body and one Spirit, just as you have been called to one glorious hope for the future.

Have you ever been here before? Asking the question "Does God even know what's happening?" I know I have. It's in moments like this where some of the best discipleship happens. Where we must lean into the arms of God and incline our ears to the voice of God to find both comfort and clarity. I believe one of the words God is "The time is now." That it's time for the church to exemplify the change, it wants to see. This is not always easy, but it's always worth it. We must make every effort to keep ourselves united in a world that so easily divides. And the church is still the hope for the future.

Reflection Questions:

Do you feel the church is engaging with culture? If not, what more could be done?

Would you be open to worshipping with persons from other ethnicities?

If so, what parts of your experience would you be willing to sacrifice?

How will you contribute to racial reconciliation within the church this week?

Inside-Out:

_____
_____
_____
_____
_____
_____
_____
_____
_____
_____
_____
_____
_____

Devotional Prayer

Lord, help my heart be open to progress. I want to bring your kingdom to the earth and show the world your love and unity. I avail myself to be a bridge to those who are different than myself. I will remain confident in my spiritual identity, but I will also remain open to your leading. I also pray that I am apart of engaging culture in every way you need. That I would not be afraid to be seen, to be heard, or to be connected where you need me for your glory. Help me live like Jesus, talk like Jesus, and engage as Jesus did. I will be apart of changing the world. In Jesus Name, Amen.

THE WHO, WHAT, WHEN, WHERE, & WHY CHAPTER
ASKING QUESTIONS IS OK

As a child, I was quite the talker in classes. Now I know that's hard to believe, but I was. On one occasion I recall my mother asking me why my test scores suffered and I said, *"I don't want to sound dumb in front of the class."* My mother's response would be embedded in my memory for the rest of my life. She said, *"The only dumb question, is the one you don't ask!"* Inherently, most people don't like feeling "out of the loop" about any topic. But the reality is you'll always have room for growth and understanding! We often face those inevitable moments when we fail to ask the questions necessary to secure a clear understanding of a particular principle or practice connected to our faith. This could be for many reasons such as lacking the effort to dig deeper in study, or the nerve to be exposed in our ignorance. Whatever the reason, it keeps us stuck in the same place of development. In this chapter, we will discuss several thoughts about asking questions that, if considered, can result in the continuous growth of your spiritual maturity.

IF YOU'RE NOT ASKING QUESTIONS, READ MORE

After doing ministry full time for years, preaching a lot of sermons, and obtaining a Masters of Divinity, it still amazes me that I see something new every time I read the Bible. Honestly, I can't read the Bible without having questions most days. This book is so full of things that take time to understand, some because they just culturally don't make sense and take historical research, others because they make us evaluate our convictions and lifestyle. But if you never have any questions about your walk, you can't be reading enough.

So here's what I suggest. When you read do three things; some which I mentioned in earlier chapters. One, ask the question how in the world does this apply to my life? That always gets my wheels turning about what I can do with the information I'm experiencing. Number two, read areas of the Bible you've never seen before! Your reading has to go beyond what Pastor preached on, stories you've already heard, and favorite scriptures. I promise you if you explore the uncharted waters of the biblical sea you will find hidden gems. Finally, read commentary or invest into a great study Bible. These will provide insight into text in ways that you never thought about from people who have often dedicated extensive study to that which you're reading. I am confident that these recommendations of reading will produce more questions. And questions are a good thing.

IF YOU DON'T HAVE ANY QUESTIONS, CHECK THE HEART

Do you remember when you first started "talking" to someone new and the excitement you experienced on those first few phone calls? For most of us, no matter our background, those conversations were filled with the same thing, questions. And it was in our questions that we found curiosity, interest, connection, and for some of us, love. Do you have that same excitement for getting to know God? Do you wake up ready to find out just a little more? Are you eager for planned moments of deeper discovery? Do you wake up early or stay up late with the intent of asking question after question to take the relationship to a deeper level? We do it for people, do you do it for God? Loving God is an experience that is relationally bound, and no relationship can continue to grow without deeper questioning. Find those questions that peak your interest in God, then go searching through the ocean of information before you. Dig deeper and deeper with hopes of getting a little closer that day. Sometimes that drive will take you to the Bible, sometimes to other people, sometimes to prayer time, but you have to dive in. Even when you don't find what you were looking for, I promise you'll find out something not only about God but about yourself. We can always identify the investment of our heart by the investment of our time!

IF YOU CAN'T FIND QUESTIONS, RELEASE FEAR

God is not afraid of your questions, and God is not upset with them either. Questions express commitment when properly presented and with the right spirit. Jesus answered the Pharisees on one occasion with these words found in *Matthew 22:37*, *"You must love the Lord your God with all your heart, all your soul, and all your mind."* Jesus says this is the greatest commandment of all. In other words, God desires not just your heart and soul, but also your mind. He wants the challenge of your intellect, reasoning, and logic. It's when you are willing to be authentic that the relationship can grow. Just for clarity, I don't believe we should challenge God's authority or power. And I'm surely not suggesting we challenge God to prove himself to us with the ultimatum of our loyalty. But God is big enough to handle the insecurities, doubts, and frustrations of our faith. Some of the greatest characters in the biblical narrative asked God questions:

Moses said *"God I don't think I'm the one."*

Gideon said, *"God my tribe is the weakest and I'm the least in my clan.."*

Joshua said *"God why did you bring us this far to destroy us"* after losing in battle to Ai.

Jesus said, *"God if there be any other way, let this cup pass me..."*

That last one always gets me! Even Jesus asked God a question! He expressed uncertainty in his process and purpose, but he took it to the greatest resource of his time and ours, God. Take the tough questions to God! Take the painful questions to God! Take the religious questions to God! He wants them, and I'd dare to say loves them. Because it's in questions that sincere desire is found. Don't run from your questions! It's in them that you'll find passion in your study, prioritization in your prayers, and purpose in your life. Every question, when asked with the right heart, can you lead us one step closer to discovering a beautiful relationship with God. In the beginning, there may be a lot of questions but fire away. Whether you're starting over or starting for the first time, enjoy the journey.

The Questions Devotional

Proverbs 18:1-2
1 A man who isolates himself seeks his own desire; He rages against all wise judgment.
2 A fool has no delight in understanding, But in expressing his own heart.

Ashley and I love trying new places to eat. Well, more-so her, but we try local restaurants in our city whenever we get the chance. One day we went to a place called Xtra's Cafe, and while the meal was great, the conversation was even better. On each table, they had a mug with hundreds of little strips of paper called conversation starters. Each a question prompting hilarious, thought-provoking, or intimate conversation. I felt a spark in our relationship that night because great questions produce great conversations, and great conversation can produce stronger commitment. It's funny how we embrace this reality in the natural but not always in the spiritual. But God is ok with our questions, and great questions are the starting point to great revelation. Don't be afraid to lean into your curiosities. Whether it's asking God or asking people, allow your questions to lead you into deeper relationship and revelation of who God is. He doesn't just want your body. He wants your mind.

Reflection Questions:

What are three questions that you'd like to explore in the coming year about your faith?

Who are three people in your life you feel comfortable exploring with and/or asking questions to in this season?

Inside-Out:

_____
_____
_____
_____
_____
_____
_____
_____
_____
_____
_____
_____
_____
_____

Devotional Prayer
This prayer is all yours to write. I pray this book has blessed you and I pray
you've found a HEAD START to a STRONG FINISH!

Made in the USA
Middletown, DE
24 January 2022

59565800R00056